BRIGHT NOTES

THE FAERIE QUEENE AND OTHER WORKS BY EDMUND SPENSER

Intelligent Education

Nashville, Tennessee

BRIGHT NOTES: The Faerie Queene and Other Works
www.BrightNotes.com

No part of this publication may be used or reproduced in any manner whatsoever without written permission, except in the case of brief quotations in critical articles and reviews. For permissions, contact Influence Publishers http://www.influencepublishers.com.

ISBN: 978-1-645420-90-3 (Paperback)
ISBN: 978-1-645420-91-0 (eBook)

Published in accordance with the U.S. Copyright Office Orphan Works and Mass Digitization report of the register of copyrights, June 2015.

Originally published by Monarch Press.
William Joseph Grace, 1963
2020 Edition published by Influence Publishers.

Interior design by Lapiz Digital Services. Cover Design by Thinkpen Designs.

Printed in the United States of America.

Library of Congress Cataloging-in-Publication Data forthcoming.
Names: Intelligent Education
Title: BRIGHT NOTES: The Faerie Queene and Other Works
Subject: STU004000 STUDY AIDS / Book Notes

CONTENTS

1)	Introduction to Edmund Spenser	1
2)	Origin and Purpose of the Work	11
3)	The Atmosphere of The Faerie Queene	22
4)	Textual Analysis	38
	Book I	38
	Book II	58
	Book III	79
	Book IV	102
	Book V	122
	Book VI	134
	The Mutability Cantos	144
5)	The Shephearde's Calender	146
6)	Daphnaida, Colin Clouts Come Home Againe, and Astrophel	152
7)	Amoretti and Epithalamion	155
8)	Prothalamion and A View of the Present State of Ireland	158

9)	Fowre Hymnes	160
10)	Critical Commentary	162
11)	Essay Questions and Answers	169
12)	Bibliography and Guide to Further Research	186

INTRODUCTION TO EDMUND SPENSER

LIFE AND ENVIRONMENT

Edmund Spenser's life, in contrast to that of a Shakespeare, offers a simple and describable pattern, on the whole well documented. He had a wide reputation as a poet in his times, and it has been maintained, with some reservations, to our own day. Born about 1552, he attended the Merchant Taylor's School, London, one of the great Humanistic schools of the English Renaissance (founded in 1561), directed, when Spenser was a student, by the famed Richard Mulcaster, who taught Hebrew, Greek, and Latin, and was seriously concerned with the improvement and development of the English language. The school had high standards of scholarship, its daily schedule running from seven in the morning to five in the afternoon. There Spenser had contact with Edmund Grindal, an examiner at the school and later Archbishop of Canterbury, to whom Spenser was to pay tribute in *The Shephearde's Calender* (1579). He proceeded to Pembroke College, Cambridge as a "sizar," one having a scholarship in return for designated services. Dr. Joseph Young was the Master of Pembroke while Spenser was in attendance; Young was later to become Bishop of Rochester, and Spenser was to be his secretary for a short time. In the above mentioned poem, Young bears the name Roffyn, and Grindal, that of Algrind. These churchmen represented the religious views with which Spenser was in sympathy and which he supported.

At Cambridge, where Spenser takes a B.A. (1573) and an M.A. (1576), he forms a life-long friendship with Gabriel Harvey, a Cambridge "don" or professor; preserved for us is a fair amount of correspondence between these men. Harvey appears as "Hobbinol" in *The Shephearde's Calender* and in *Colin Clouts Come Home Againe* (1595). After a brief service in the household of Robert Dudley, Earl of Leicester (whom Spenser deeply admired - he is reflected in the person of Arthur in *The Faerie Queene*, and a special tribute is to be found in the "Prothalamion", 1596), he becomes secretary to Lord Grey of Wilton (Artegall in *The Faerie Queene*), who had just been appointed Lord Deputy of Ireland (1580).

SPENSER'S POLITICAL ALIGNMENT

In 1579 Spenser published *The Shephearde's Calender*, a series of pastoral eclogues organized according to the months of the year, with a special commentary by one Edward Kirke. This deliberately enigmatic work will be discussed elsewhere. Praised by Sir Philip Sidney in the *Defence of Poesie* (in manuscript about 1580), and by others, this work underlines Spenser's alignment with Leicester, Sir Philip Sidney (Calidore in *The Faerie Queene*), Sir Francis Walsingham (Meliboe in *The Faerie Queene*) in opposing a proposed marriage between Queen Elizabeth with the Duc d'Alencon, younger brother of the French King. This proposed match, for some time a matter of touch-and-go, alarmed many influential persons, though it had the support of William Cecil, Lord Burghley, the Queen's Treasurer and long-time adviser. Spenser's feelings can be measured by the fact that the clownish Braggadocchio in *The Faerie Queene* stands for Alencon, and the sly Trompart for Simier, his ambassador. A recent scholarly work, Paul McLane's Spenser's *Shephearde's Calender: A Study in Elizabeth Allegory*, sees the opposition to this marriage as a central **theme** of the *Calender*.

Spenser, in a subordinate capacity, knows the great men of his day and is always on the outskirts of great events. As far as his own advancement is concerned, he did well, but could have done much better. The man who effectively stops the progress of Spenser's career is Lord Burghley, whom Spenser attacks in "Mother Hubberd's Tale" for nepotism, feathering his own nest, and caring nothing for art and scholarship. ("Mother Hubberd's Tale" was published in 1591, but was probably written about 1580.)

SPENSER'S LIFE IN IRELAND

Spenser spent the last eighteen years of his life in Ireland, with one interruption of about two years (1590-91) during which he returned to England in the company of the adventurer-courtier, Sir Walter Raleigh (Timias in *The Faerie Queene*). There was another visit to England in 1595 or 1596. He held a succession of posts. Appointed in March, 1581, he held the post of Clerk of the Chancery for Faculties for seven years. He became in 1585 the deputy to Lodowick Bryskett (the author of A Discourse of Civil Life, Containing the Ethic Part of Moral Friendship, which gave an account of Spenser's project with regard to *The Faerie Queene*) in the post of the clerkship of the Council of Munster. In 1589, succeeded Bryskett in the post. In 1585 he also became a prebendary of Limerick Cathedral, an office with nominal duties to which a stipend was attached. Kilcolman Castle, with 3028 acres, situated between Limerick to the north and Cork to the south, was assigned to Spenser in 1586 (the formal grant coming in 1590). This was part of the more than 500,000 acres forfeited by the Earl of Desmond, after the final failure of his insurrection in 1586. Sir Walter Raleigh had been granted a "seignory" of about 12,000 acres thirty miles away. The new holders of dispossessed lands were known as "undertakers," and they were supposed to bring a stated number of English families to settle on these estates within a given period of time. Sir Walter Raleigh, temporarily out of favor at court, tool occasion to visit his new Irish estate in 1589. Himself a poet, as well as an explorer and tough fighting man, Raleigh had the opportunity to hear Spenser recite the completed sections of *The Faerie Queene*. In the autumn of 1589, Spenser and Sir Walter Raleigh sail back to England together (the journey and the subsequent effects of the visit to the Court of Elizabeth are described in *Colin Clouts Come Home Againe*, 1595).

What were the conditions of Spenser's life in Ireland, and what was his reaction to them? On the financial side, we must become used to the difference in meaning attached to sums of money in Spenser's time and in our own. On February 25, 1591, Spenser was granted a pension for life of 50 pounds, in recognition of the presentation of the first three books of *The Faerie Queene* to Elizabeth. At today's current rate of exchange, this is somewhat less than $150.00 But Spenser paid a rental of only 22 pounds a year for his vast Kilcolman estate! His yearly salary as secretary to Lord Grey had been 20 pounds! Bishop John Whitgift pointed out in 1585 that over half the benefices in England paid less than 10 pounds a year. Elizabeth Boyle, who married Spenser in June, 1594, brought a considerable dowry into the marriage-250 pounds! Spenser was a poor man by comparison with the great English feudal lords whose practically unlimited resources were constantly being increased by sequestrations of Church property. But by ordinary standards, Spenser was at no time poverty-stricken.

From repeated statements in his work (he has a long account of the countryside about Arlo-hill and "old father Mole" in the first of the Mutability Cantos, as well as detailed references in *Colin Clouts Come Home Againe* and in the "Epithalamion"), Spenser was in love with the countryside surrounding his castle. The castle stood on rising ground amid the Ballyhoura hills, which were watered by the crystals streams of the Bregog and the Awbeg, which ran through forests and cleared land. In fact, Spenser loved everything about his Irish home, except the Irish!

CONDITIONS IN IRELAND

The historical, social, and economic conditions of Ireland were deplorable. It has been estimated that 30,000 men, women, and children had perished as a result of the Desmond insurrection. Spenser had been an eye-witness to military operations while in the service of Lord Grey, who had been recalled in August, 1582, partly because Elizabeth did not approve of the severity of his methods. Spenser certainly did; his gentle, humanistic Platonism fell short when it came to dealing with the Irish. In *A View of the Present State of Ireland* (written about 1596, publication withheld until 1633), Spenser approves of using the sword and famine as instruments of setting up a foundation on which better things might be built. In that long prose dialogue, he describes human beings creeping on their hands out of corners of the woods and glens because their legs were too weak to support them. They looked like "anatomies of death." They sounded like ghosts crying out from their graves; they were happy if they could find carrion to eat. They struggled to find water-cress or shamrock. Spenser adds "that in short space there were almost none left, and a most populous and plentiful country suddenly made void of man and beast." Spenser looked upon the Irish as savages; his description of Maleger's forces

(*The Faerie Queene*, II. xi) may very well reflect his opinion of them, and Talus, the iron man, in Book V of *The Faerie Queene*, may well indicate Spenser's indifference to Irish survival.

If horror and beauty are the mixed ingredients of *The Faerie Queene*, they but reflect Spenser's own environment in Ireland. Spenser's charming, romantic, feudal domain was to be laid waste by a Maleger with fire and sword when there was no Talus with an iron flail to save it.

SPENSER'S CONNECTIONS

In regard to another aspect of Spenser's life, his affiliation with some of the great courtiers and ladies of his time, we have a mixed picture of inspiration and frustration. Spenser is a kinsman of Sir John Spenser of Althorp, and is particularly devoted to Sir John's three influential daughters:

.............the sisters three, The honor of the noble familie Of which I meanest boast my selfe to be... (*Colin Clouts Come Home Againe*, 536-8)

To Elizabeth, Lady Carey, Spenser dedicated "Muiopotmos"; to Anne, Lady Compton and Mountegle, "Mother Hubberd's Tale": to Alice, Lady Strange (later, wife of Lord Ellesmere, the Lord Chancellor), the "Tears of the Muses". The last is the Lady Egerton before whom Milton's *Arcades* was produced when she was an elderly lady. All of these poems appear in *Complaints Containing Sundre Small Poems of the World's Vanitie* (1591). Besides his intimate knowledge of the society and relatives connected with the Earl of Leicester (died, 1588), and with Sir Philip Sidney (died 1586), Spenser was acquainted with many others of high station and he lists them under disguised names in *Colin Clouts Come Home Againe*. There can be no doubt about the depth and breadth of Spenser's connections, but on several occasions Spenser expresses deep regrets about the practical results of these connections. He lives in an age when a cultivated humanist, a poet and rhetorician, might reasonably expect to rise to high office within the "patronage" system. Ariosto and Tasso had been highly honored by the aristocratic houses which they had praised in their epics, and perhaps Spenser believed that he had fallen short of the honor that was due him. But certainly at no point does he breathe a word of criticism about Queen Elizabeth. Even allowing for the extravagances of Renaissance rhetoric, Spenser pulls all the stops in praise of her. It may have been a psychological necessity for Spenser to believe all that he said about her; it was his essential article of faith. Spenser could be a biting satirist; he had a strain of ruthlessness about him, as can be seen in his attitude toward the Irish, and which is indirectly indicated in sections of *The Faerie Queene*. But Elizabeth is perfection absolute. She has all the authority of a religious symbol as well as being head of a secular state. The theory of "Divine Right" - that a ruler receives his authority directly from God over his people, and is answerable to no one but God - is everywhere implicitly accepted by Spenser.

SPENSER'S VIEW OF THE COURT

Consequently, in his disappointments, Spenser never blames Elizabeth for not doing enough for him, but rather the court. In *Colin Clouts Come Home Againe*, Colin Clout (Spenser's pseudonym, symbolizing the true, honest Anglo-Saxon Englishman) berates the shamelessness and immorality of the court. He rejects the great medieval game of courtly love, with its mistresses, "servants," peculiar kinds of courtesy and honor, and frequent adultery. He is disgusted with the mad competitive scramble for "favors" and advancement. At court there is no respect for art or scholarship; people are judged by the clothes they wear and the attitudes they strike.

Ne any there doth brave or valiant seeme, Unlesse that some gay mistresse badge he beares: Ne any one himselfe doth ought esteeme, Unlesse he swim in love up to the eares. (*Colin Clouts Come Home Againe*, 776-80)

Spenser compares the court unfavorably with the simple rural life he leads back in Ireland! Elizabeth is an inspiration, but the court is frustration and worse. Hobbinol (Gabriel Harvey), who partakes in the dialogue, tries to persuade Spenser to take a more moderate view. But this poem indicates that as much as Spenser may have disliked the Irish, he hardly regarded Ireland as a Siberia.

THE FAERIE QUEENE AND SPENSER'S MARRIAGE

The first three books of *The Faerie Queene* are published during his London visit, of 1590, and he obtains readings with the Queen. His *Complaints*, including a wide selection of pieces, are brought out in the next year, 1591. After returning to Ireland, he marries Elizabeth Boyle in June, 1594. (There is some question about the date.) According to tradition, Spenser wrote the "Epithalamion" in his bride's honor, in lieu of the wedding presents which failed to arrive from London on time. Many believe the "Epithalamion" to be the most ecstatic and enchanting of all Spenser's poetry. Elizabeth was Spenser's second wife. (By his first wife, Machabyas Childe, he had two children, Sylvanus and Katherine.) By his second wife he is to have a son named Peregrine (the name signifying a foreigner, one coming from abroad). The "Epithalamion", together with a

sonnet sequence, "Amoretti", which may have been connected with his courtship, was published in 1595.

The year 1596 saw the installment of the next three books of *The Faerie Queene*. Published in the same year are the *Fowre Hymnes* in honor of Love, of Beauty, of Heavenly Love, and of Heavenly Beauty. A new edition is brought out of the "Daphnaida", which was first printed in 1591, and the first three books of *The Faerie Queene* undergo their second printing.

DISASTER STRIKES

Spenser continues to lead the life of a landed gentleman, feuding at law over property rights with his neighbor Lord Roche, purchasing an estate for his son, Peregrine. In September, 1598, he is given the important office of Sheriff of Cork. But Spenser is not allowed to forget that he is living in frontier country, however idyllic it might appear. Like Pastorella's country in Book VI of *The Faerie Queene*, it is open to savage and unexpected attack. In 1598 the long and dangerous rebellion of Tyrone O'Neill breaks out. In October of that year Kilcolman castle is "sacked." Spenser and the other "undertakers" take refuge in the walled town of Cork. The story told by Ben Jonson that Spenser lost a child in the destruction of the castle is no longer credited by scholars, and the belief that the remaining six books of *The Faerie Queene* may have been also lost in this way is a pure guess.

SPENSER'S DEATH

Spenser arrived in London on Christmas Eve, 1598, bearing a message from the Governor of Munster to the privy Council, for which service he was paid 8 pounds. In less than a monthon January 16, 1599, Spenser was dead. He was buried in Westminster Abbey, near the grave of Chaucer. The Earl of Essex paid the expenses of the funeral. Obviously there is no foundation for Jonson's story that Spenser died of starvation in a garret.

Such are the bald facts. They do not indicated the ways in which Spenser assimilated the baroque lushness of the Renaissance, how he brought about a combination of images in his poetry from many kinds of tradition, as if everything could be "synthesized" and united. A journey with Sir Walter Raleigh sounds trivial, but here Spenser is in contact with a man who opened the western continents, the founder of Virginia, the freebooter of the Spanish main. Here is Spenser, in his associations with leading noblemen and churchmen, close to the main developments in Church and State. Spenser's concern with the threat of Spain, his serious moral and religious values, leaning a little to the left of the Elizabethan religious compromise, are all connected with an active involvement in the affairs of his day. But, fortunately for the artist, he was not too involved. His Irish "exile" must also have given him, especially in the surroundings of Kilcolman castle, some time to think, brood, and dream.

THE FAERIE QUEENE

ORIGIN AND PURPOSE OF THE WORK

The Faerie Queene is first mentioned in a letter of Edmund Spenser to Gabriel Harvey, dated April, 1580. Spenser asks Harvey for his judgment and criticism of the partly finished manuscript he is sending him. We have Harvey's reply; he was not very enthusiastic. Spenser's making a mistake, he says, in trying to compete with Ariosto's Orlando Furioso. Hobgoblin (a general term for the "faery" world) has run away with the garland of Apollo (a symbol of poetry). In other words, Harvey felt that Spenser had sacrificed his poetic genius to a far-fetched, unreal world.

We also have a document giving an account by Spenser of his own work. This is contained in Lodowick Bryskett's A Discourse of Civil Life, written before 1589, though not published until 1606. The subject matter of the book is "the ethical part of Moral Philosophy." It is dedicated to Arthur. late Lord Grey of Wilton, possibly before this official's recall from Ireland in 1582. An account is given of the conversation of a group of men, including Spenser, who had been Lord Grey's secretary, at a meeting in Bryskett's cottage near Dublin.

Bryskett feels that the Italians have done a wonderful job in clarifying the ideas of Plato and Aristotle, and of expressing these ideas in the language of Italy. He wishes that English writers would do a similar service for England and the English language. Bryskett points to Spenser in the group as "not only perfect in the Greek tongue, but also very well read in philosophy, both moral and natural." He wants Spenser to address the group on the benefits to be obtained from the knowledge of moral philosophy, to define it, to point out its various parts, to distinguish virtues (these distinctions were to form a great deal of the material of *The Faerie Queene*). Spenser, in reply, then excuses himself before the group in not undertaking to do this, because (to use own quoted words) "I have already undertaken a work tending to the same effect, which is in heroical verse under the title of a Faerie Queene to represent all the moral virtues, assigning to every virtue a Knight to be the patron and defender of the same, in whose actions and feats of arms and chivalry the operations of that virtue, whereof he is the protector, are to be expressed, and the vices and unruly appetites that oppose themselves against the same, to be beaten down and overcome."

The most explicit statement of Spenser's intentions in *The Faerie Queene* is addressed to the colorful Sir Walter Raleigh, elegant courtier, fighting sea captain, poet, historian, founder of Virginia, in a letter of January, 1589. Raleigh was an extravagant enough figure, except perhaps for his hard-headed **realism**, to be himself a character in *The Faerie Queene!* Spenser says he is going to "discover" (reveal) the meaning of this continued allegory or "dark conceite" to his friend, who had visited Spenser at Kilcolman castle in Ireland in 1589. Spenser is aware of how "doubtfully" allegories may be "construed," and here he at least makes clear his general allegorical outline.

THE IMAGE OF A GENTLEMAN

The over-all purpose is to give us, as we would say today, the "image" of "a gentleman or noble person in virtuous and gentle discipline." Spenser's historical period, that of the Renaissance, was greatly concerned with the idea of the "gentleman." This was a sort of humanistic parallel to the medieval idea of the "saint," but with certain changes suited to the new spirit of the times. There was much less tendency in Spenser's day than in medieval times to make a drastic opposition between "the world" and "the spirit." The "world," in spite of its evil and tragedy, was seen as a beautiful, exciting place, evidence of God's creative power. As they expressed it then, people were interested in reading "the Book of God's Works," as well as "the Book of God's Words." Man, therefore, should be trained both in "Works" and "Words" - while remaining religiously reverent, he should try to be accomplished as a scholar, soldier, courtier. Always a good Christian, he nevertheless should know and appreciate the world, and use it wisely and well.

Accompanying this idea was the concept of the "complete man." John Milton, who thinks of Spenser as "sage" and "serious," a better teacher than Scotus or Aquinas, views the liberal education as the means for making a man fit for any office, private or public, in peace or war. This is the humanist ideal, which, in our own age of specialization, has become somewhat dimmed. It is this ideal of a completed perfection in all the essential areas of life that Spenser elaborates in his letter to Raleigh.

The virtuous man is, in the thought of the day, primarily one who knows how to govern himself, and, therefore, is equipped to govern others. Spenser states that Homer, in his portrait of Ulysses and Virgil in his Aeneas, depicted "the good governor and virtuous man."

ETHICAL AND POLITICAL VIRTUES

But Spenser goes on to make a distinction, important for understanding his thought, between "ethical" virtues and "political" virtues. This distinction had a lot of impact on Renaissance thinking. The twelfth century medieval commentator on Aristotle, Averroes, had set forth the theory of the "double truth." Something might be quite true in philosophy, but false in theology - and also the other way around. In Machiavelli's notorious The Prince, this point of view coincides with a distinction between "ethics" as private morality and "politics" as public morality. Machiavelli allows many things to the Prince as morally permissible ("politics") which he would regard as wicked in the individual ("Ethics"). Machiavelli would not have understood the moralist's condemnation of his doctrine that "the end justifies the means." For Machiavelli public morality (the "safety of the State") followed different principles from those of private life. A king could liquidate his political enemies, but a private citizen may not shoot down his neighbors.

Spenser's thinking on this matter is different from that of a Machiavelli and nearer the original Aristotle. Though Aristotle grants (Politics, III, iv) that "the good citizen may not be a good man; the good citizen is one who does good service to his state, and the state may be bad in principle," he also says (Politics, III, ix) that the true object of the state is virtue. Like Spenser, Aristotle identifies the good man and the good ruler. "Since the good ruler is the same as the good man, our education must be so framed as to produce the good man" (Politics, VII, xiv).

Spenser, in following the **epic** tradition of poetry, is trying to teach as well as give pleasure. The **epic** was traditionally a narrative work recited by a court poet for an aristocratic audience, and, in the Renaissance, was used in the education of young future rulers by illustrating wise political "know-how" and "courtesy" (today we would call it good "public relations"). Always present in Spenser's work is this instructional angle, which gave the Elizabethans great pleasure, but with which we may be unfamiliar.

THE CONCEPT OF VIRTUE

It remains to ask, in regard to this famed letter to Sir Walter Raleigh, what Spenser meant by "virtue" and what particular virtues he intended to deal with.

Spenser follows the Aristotelian idea of virtue as a "mean" between "extremes," between "excesses" and "deficiencies." Again and again, he presents stories and **episodes** which illustrate his concept of a virtue by depicting its corresponding vices, the excesses and deficiencies that are opposed to it. Then he emphatically drives home his positive meaning, the true virtue that avoids these extremes. We shall have frequent cause to note this in our analysis of the contents of the various books of *The Faerie Queene*.

Aristotle's statement in the Nicomachean Ethics, II, ix, outlines precisely the problem that fascinated Spenser. "That moral virtue is a mean, then, and in what sense it is so, and that is a mean between two vices, the one involving excess, the other deficiency, and that it is such because its character is to aim at what is intermediate in passion and actions, has been sufficiently stated. Hence it is no easy task to be good. For in everything it is no easy task to find the middle, e.g. to find the middle of the circle is not for everyone but for him who knows; so, too, anyone can get angry - that is easy - or to give or spend money; but to do this to the right person, to the right extent, at the right time with the right motive, and in the right way, that is not for everyone, nor is it easy; wherefore goodness is both rare and laudable and noble."

Thus, for Aristotle, the virtue of courage is a mean between rashness (an extreme of excess) and cowardice (an extreme of deficiency). Similarly with the other virtues: temperance is a mean between self-indulgence and insensibility; liberality, a mean between prodigality and meanness; magnificence, a mean between vulgarity and niggardness; friendliness, a mean between obsequiousness and churlishness; truthfulness, a mean between boastfulness and mock modesty.

In the central character of Arthur, before he was king, Spenser was to image a man, perfected in the twelve moral virtues "as Aristotle hath devised." This was to be done in the first twelve books (actually only six were completed, though we have part of a seventh). Spenser was even more ambitious; he had the intention of undertaking another work of equal magnitude, illustrating the political virtues in Arthur after he became king.

What are virtues that are actually stressed in the work that Spenser has given us, only part of the original design? We see almost at once that they only very roughly parallel those of Aristotle.

GLORY

The first he mentions is that of glory. "Glory" was a Renaissance preoccupation. It meant fame, reputation, the pursuit of an eminent and undying achievement - the sort of thing Milton, who was the last great heir of this tradition, had in mind when he spoke of Fame:

Fame is the spur that the clear spirit doth raise (That last infirmity of noble mind) To scorn delights and live laborious days...

Milton, considering fame here only within a worldly context, thinks of it as a kind of noble infirmity rather than a virtue. True fame is a plant that does not grow on mortal soil. The sense of glory as a driving objective in the individual had been stimulated by the Renaissance zeal for the ancient classics. Bowra in The Greek Experience points out that Achilles, the formidable Greek warrior, "complains not that he is fated to die young, but that too much of his life is spoiled by misfortunes which hinder his pursuit of glory. In the thought of glory most Greeks found a consolation for the shadowy doom which awaited them in the grave."

Spenser, like Milton, has Christianized the pagan sense of glory. While not forgetting its worldly aspect, he keeps in mind the kind of glory associated with the medieval saint, what the Puritans meant by "glorification" following upon "election and sanctification."

In his own words - "In that Faery Queens I mean glory in my general intention, but in my particular I conceive the most excellent and glorious person of our sovereign the Queen..." Queen Elizabeth of England, who is the embodiment of this universal and inclusive virtue, is "shadowed" or reflected in other female characters.

Spenser's allegory presents a small problem here. The virtuous man or woman is one, a complete person. But in the stories of the different personages, one virtue is emphasized more than the others. But beyond these figures an over-riding character is presented who is meant to symbolize all the moral strengths of the individuals summed up in one, Gloriana, for example, or Prince Arthur.

MAGNIFICENCE

Prince Arthur represents "Magnificence." This virtue, Spenser says, is the perfection of all the rest, and contains in it them all. How is it, then, to be distinguished from "Glory" about which the same might be said? Chaucer spoke of his Knight as possessing "freedom," by which he meant the qualities of a truly great person, the opposite of anything base or ignoble. Other medieval writers used the word "largesse" in somewhat the same sense. The truly great person is generous, openhearted, far from what is petty and suspicious. "Freedom," largesse, magnificence are the characteristics of the man who possesses all the virtues, and has gone beyond any one of them. But some distinction remains between "Magnificence" and "Glory," though they cover the same ground. Magnificence means the possession of greatness, it means greatness in action. Glory means greatness too, but in the sense of something already achieved and universally recognized. In simple language, we might say that Gloriana has "arrived," but that Prince Arthur is getting there! Magnificence does not involve the idea of reputation. Glory does.

ARISTOTLE TRANSFORMED

Too much had happened in European culture since the time of Aristotle for Spenser merely to reaffirm Aristotle's classification of the virtues. Throughout Spenser's work the concept of Christian Grace is pervasive. No less foreign to Aristotle than the various knights with their "emblematic" shields(Sir Guyon with the image of the Faerie Queens, Sir Scudamour with that of Cupid,

Sir Sanglier with a broken sword against a background of blood) would be a compound virtue such as "Courtesy" in Book VI. This concept of courtesy incorporates a number of Aristotelian ideas but transcends them by union with the Christian concept of charity-a powerful idea that is post-Aristotelian, and is now also associated in the Renaissance with a long cultural history of knightly etiquette.

Of the six books of *The Faerie Queene* that we have, only three correspond fairly closely to Aristotle's system in their thematic virtues. Temperance (Book II), Friendship (Book IV), Justice (Book V) have much in common with Aristotle's approach. But Holiness (Book I), Chastity (Book III), Courtesy (Book VI) have special dimensions, largely due to the Christian view of Divine Grace, that mark a radical departure from Aristotelian concepts and, in an indirect way, contrast with the Greek sense of the mean as "moderation." Can holiness, for example, be moderate?

THE ALLEGORICAL METHOD

What exactly does Spenser mean by the continued allegory and "dark conceite" in regard to *The Faerie Queene?* First of all we should recognize the common Renaissance argument supporting the cause of poetry. Sir Philip Sidney in An Apology for Poetry (1595) stated that poetry was a "speaking picture" with the aim of teaching and delighting. It combined the advantages of history, dealing with specific particulars, and of philosophy, dealing with universal principles, with its own special pictorial (or "imagistic") effectiveness. Spenser's view is parallel to this. While he grants that many would prefer to have their philosophy "strait," he finds it much more "profitable" and "gracious" to use the imaginative pictorial methods of poetry.

But, of course, poetry does not have to be allegorical. Here we must recognize that allegorical communication was much more a normal method of communication in Medieval and Renaissance times than it is today. In the Middle Ages, every animal and every plant signified something beyond itself. The pelican feeding its young symbolized Christ; the lion on public buildings was the Lion of Judah, representing Christ in another aspect, that of strength. Often a single image was used as the sign of a complicated idea. Thus the loss of the "Pearl" in the famous medieval poem by that name represented "spiritual dryness," a loss of the sense of satisfaction in the religious life. Often further constructions are made on the basis of a traditional symbol as, in this example, on the pearl "of great price" in the Scripture, for which the trader sold his lesser peals. In *The Faerie Queene*, Book I, Una's lion represents the strength of truth through the "natural" law, as Una herself personifies revealed truth. As Henry Taylor observes, "Medieval thought tended to symbolism and to move from symbol to symbol, and from symbolical significance to related significance, and often indeed to treat a symbol as if it were the fact which was symbolized." This tradition goes way back into the past, to the embodiment of abstract qualities in the classical gods, and in even more obvious figures such as Concord and Fortune. Scriptural commentary, particularly on the Old Testament, had viewed the narration of events as "pre-figurings," as allegories of what was to happen later (the so-called "anagogic" method). Even more important in forming the tradition of allegory was the "tropological" commentary, in which the scriptural text was used to offer a moral significance apart from the direct meaning. Thus, in one case (the anagogic), the story of Jonah in the whale's belly would typify the death and resurrection of Christ, the "harrowing of hell" - Christ's release of the souls in Limbo. In the other (the tropological), the story of Abraham and Isaac would be used to drive home the thesis of unquestioned obedience to the will of God.

It is not to far-fetched to say that medieval and Renaissance readers were as much at home with the allegorical method as we are today with factual reporting, "inside" stories based on research. Our problem is to recover for ourselves what have been aptly termed "lost metaphors" - that is, the allegorical significance that was once universally attached to certain names and incidents. Thus Milton's Samson Agonistes is more basically about the Passion of Christ than it is about Samson himself. Samson traditionally "pre-figured" Christ, for he was a "Nazar" a man whose birth was in some sense extraordinary or miraculous (Samson was born to a woman past the child-bearing age), a man dedicated to God in a special way from his mother's womb, who had to live under even stricter religious rules than other Hebrews. This was all well known to seventeenth century readers, but today we have to be told about it.

Hazlitt once said that we could enjoy *The Faerie Queene* without letting the allegory "bite" us. This is only very roughly true. Allegorical meaning is basic and primary to the whole work. But Spenser operates on several levels of allegory at the same time. Thus a character might represent a rather carefully defined abstract quality, a national political situation, a specific individual whom Spenser personally knew. Not all these representations are equally important or equally clear. But since *The Faerie Queene* is primarily a treatise in moral philosophy, the first level of the allegory (that of abstract qualities) is essential to the understanding of the work.

THE FAERIE QUEENE

THE ATMOSPHERE OF THE FAERIE QUEENE

What sort of a world is that of *The Faerie Queene?* The first impression is that of an endless tapestry of picture metaphors, replete with beautiful wooded landscapes, with springs and rivers and shaded clearings away from the sun, where nymphs and goddesses can casually be met. It is also a world of fantastic, nightmarish and hideous monsters, of barbarous cruelties, of the clash of steel on steel, with blood oozing on the green meadow, limbs and heads lopped off, of people racing about hysterically, pursuing or pursued. All myths and mythology are mingled, and the reader is prepared to meet anything. The prevailing texture is medieval - the knight mounted on his horse, the tournament, the castle, the dungeon, the dragon, the palmer, the hermit, the beautiful lady in distress. But at any moment the reader may find himself amid the deities of ancient times, or in a "masque" of allegorical figures that were never found before on sea or land. The landscape is prevailingly English, but the reader may find himself in a desert wilderness or beside the raging sea, and meet wild boars, lions, leopards, and a blatant beast or two.

The work has a dream-like rather than a logical quality, in spite of the fact that the allegories follow a carefully pre-arranged plan. There is plenty of action in the work. As Pauline Parker says, "those who have a vague idea of (Spenser's) narrative as a dreamy, dragging thing, where nothing much happens under the shadow of mighty trees, have certainly not counted up all the alarums and excursions which are crowded into so short a space." While this is undoubtedly true, action is not the predominant impression of the work. The words that perhaps best describe it are "masque" and "tableau."

A "masque" was a favorite entertainment of the Elizabethan court; it featured an allegorical struggle between the forces of good and evil, expressed in dialogue, song, and dance (with audience participation). The sort of thing that we are acquainted with in the Mardi Gras or the Tournament of Roses at Pasadena, with their many "figurative" floats, echoes the customs of Elizabethan times. Not only in the masque, which had a unifying, dramatic thread running through it, but in various public ceremonies and receptions, the Elizabethans were habituated to the "live" impersonation of allegorical abstractions without their being set in a story. They were familiar with what we have come to call the "tableau" - the striking scene which delivers a message, and then fades into the background without exciting us in the way that a tragedy or a comedy do. One of Spenser's problems, as fine a narrative artist as he is, is that the right allegorical figures are always bound to win, however horrible may be their temporary setbacks. He cannot permit the more moving and lacerating effects of tragedy, where the "good" and "right" character ends in defeat, at least in temporal life as we know it. Where tragic possibility is present, the reader is more concerned and emotionally involved. When the allegorical method demands the ultimate victory of virtue, the reader is apt to be more relaxed; in fact, he is watching masque and tableau, interesting as these may be in themselves.

Another reason for the dream-like aspect of *The Faerie Queene* is a certain nostalgic quality, a longing to recapture the past. This was already present in Sir Thomas Malory's Morte d'Arthur, a work to which Spenser is partly indebted. Malory testified that the age of Chivalry was already past, after the slaughterous Wars of the Roses, when he said that the object of his work was to restore "the ancient pattern of Chivalry." One does not attempt to restore something that is still alive. Spenser, more than a hundred years later, echoes Malony's appetite for the past.

O! goodly usage of those antique tymes, In which the sword was servaunt unto right; When not for malice and contentious crymes, But all for prayse, and proofe of manly might, The martial brood accustomed to fight: Then honour was the meed of victory... (III, i, xiii)

THE MEDIEVAL SETTING

What are the **conventions** of the medieval setting? The framework of each book is that of an "adventure" of a "Knight-errant." An adventure implies a dangerous commitment, in which, if the knight is successful, his moral stature and reputation are enhanced. Theoretically, he may be killed, but the one thing he must avoid is dishonor. He is called "errant" in the Latin sense of "traveling," of being sent on a mission.

The ideal knighthood had been reverenced for centuries. St. Louis, thirteenth century King of France, once told Master Robert, founder of the University of Paris, that to be a worthy knight was such a great and good thing that merely to name it filled one's mouth. Largesse (or "magnifence") was the knight's ultimate quality, outweighing courage, hardihood, high station, and noble birth. Religious faith and personal "fealty" (loyalty) distinguished the true knight. When invested with knighthood, he swore to renounce the pursuit of material gain; to do nobly for the mere love of nobleness; to be courteous to the vanquished; to redress wrongs, to be generous of his goods. "The investiture of a knight was no less a true consecration to high unselfish aims for life than was the ordination of a priest."

At one time the knight had real social and economic power, before the revolution had taken place in military tactics through the use of batteries of archers and the invention of gunpowder. Heavily armed in armor and on horseback, he outmatched all but fellow knights. In the chronicles of Froissart (thirteenth century) we get a good idea of the medieval knightly code. Equal rank fights equal rank according to strict **conventions** of honor. The defeated knight is spared his life, if he assures "fealty" to the victor, becomes "his" man.

By Spenser's time, even by Malory's, the knight had ceased to be the pivotal figure in the hierarchical socio-economic structure of feudalism in which the landowner held his lands in return for organizing defenses and rendering active military service. Though the ideals of knighthood were perpetuated (as in the person of Sir Philip Sidney, whom Spenser deeply admired), the knight was as much part of contemporary Elizabethan life as the frontier cowboy of the "Westerns" is of ours today. He had become a romanticized literary figure, and, in the example of Britomart, we even have a lady knight!

Spenser says of the errant knight (III, i, xiv) that it truly is no longer easy to know where on earth, or how, he may be found:

For he ne wonneth in one certain stead, But restlesse walketh all the world arownd, As doing thinge that to his fame redownd, Defending Ladies cause and Orphans right, Whereso he heares that any doth confownd Them comfortlesse through tyranny or might: So is his soveraine honour raisde to hevens hight.

Although these "derring-doers" are often "wrapt in fetters of a golden tress" (Spenser specializes in blondes), their main driving urge is that of fame:

Most sacred fyre, that burnest mightily In living brests, ykindled first above Emongst th'eternal spheres and lamping sky, And thence pourd into men, which men call Love! Not that same, which doth base affections move In brutish mindes, and filthy lusts inflame, But that sweete fit that doth true beautie love, And choseth vertue for his dearest Dame, Whence spring all noble deedes and never dying fame: (III, i, i)

This "eternal brood of glorie Excellent" (I, v, i) might well ask "is ought on earth so precious or so dear as praise and honor?" (V, xl, lxii).

The derring-doers win the rewards of undying fame by fighting a fierce collection of weird monsters, giants, dragons, magicians, and plain mean, tough "traitor" and "miscreant" opponent knights. As in our own "Westerns," the horses are seldom damaged, and Spenser observes

But chiefly skill to ride seems a science Proper to gentle blood...

But the grassy ground is apt to be a deep sanguine after the knights have finished with one another. A knight swerves, and his opponent breaks his lance in his thigh, leaving the head:

Out of the wound the red blood flowed fresh, That underneath his feet soone made a purple plesh.

Fallen knights "wallow" in their own gore. Spenser has no restraint in his vivid descriptions of the horrors of personal combat.

Nor does Spenser hesitate to pile on nauseating and repulsive details in describing some of his allegorical figures. Duessa, defeated and unmasked, is thus described:

But at her rompe she growing had behind A foxes taile, with dong all fowly dight.

The Red Cross Knight fights Error, half woman, half serpent. As a symbol of her perverted fertility

She poured forth out of her hellish sinke Her fruitful cursed spawne of serpents small, Deformed monsters, fowle, and black as ink.

After Error has been mortally wounded,

They flocked all about her bleeding wound, And sucked up their dying mother's blood, Making her death their life...

A good deal of *The Faerie Queene* is a counterpoint of beauty and horror. Violent and terrifying events occur in this fairy land, but they are subordinated, as in Milton's Comus, to the over-all **theme** that "virtue gives herself light through darkness for to wade." (I, i, xii).

THE POEM AS AFFIRMATION

Though Spenser occasionally expresses pessimism, as in the legend of Astraea at the beginning of Book V, he never, even in this case, has any doubt that right will win in the end. His pessimism takes the form of comparing the present unfavorably with the past, but he believes that the present can always be made better, particularly under his patroness, Queen Elizabeth.

Astraea (Latin feminine for "star") was the goddess who frequented all mankind in the golden age, representing truth, concord, justice. When something went wrong in the world, when the golden age slipped into the silver age, Astraea visited only chosen individuals and only under the cover of darkness. In the age of iron, when war, enmity, and jealousy prevailed among men, she ceased making any visits whatever. Virgil, in his celebrated Fourth Eclogue, predicted the return of the golden age, foretold that the stars and planets would return to the positions in the heavens they occupied then, and prophesied that the Virgin (Astraea) would return to a restored world. But Spenser is not so sure:

Me seemes the world is runne quite out of square From the first point of his appointed source, And being once amisse, grows daily wourse and wourse. (V, Prologue, i)

He adds

For from the golden age, that first was named, It's now at earst become a stone...

The stars have wandered much in the last few thousand years. But for all that, Sir Artegall ("Justice") is now the invigorated servant of Astraea:

And all the depth of rightfull doome was taught By fair Astraea, with great industrie, Whilest here on earth she lived mortallie. (V, i, v)

Spenser's land of Faerie has a shifting time relationship. It is under the patronage of Queen Elizabeth; its justice is administered by Sir Artegall (Lord Grey of Wilton). Its evils are universal and of all time. But its virtues and courage often have a distant and antique air. We must remember here, of course, the Renaissance habit of using history as analogy, and as "example" for the present times. The ideal side of the Faerie land does not necessarily exist in the Elizabethan present, although Spenser desires that it should. It was in the goodly usage of the antique times that "the sword was servant unto right."

It is an ideal world with which Spenser is primarily concerned. This is a world where Britomart, "glorious mirror of celestial grace," can encourage Scudamore by saying that a life is not lost, by which is won endless renown, renown "more than death, is to be sought." It is a land where the virtues are linked in a "goodly golden chain"

And noble mindes of yore allyed were In brave poursuitt of chevalrous emprize... (I, ix, i)

But even the "Faerie lond" is a "fallen" world; it is a world of struggle and trial, but with an insistent memory of an innocent, natural state - of "untroubled nature" that "doth her selfe suffise," of an "antique" world:

The antique world in his first flowring youth Fownd no defect in his Creators grace... (II, vii, xvi)

While individual daring has the primary emphasis, all is ultimately dependent on Grace:

Ne let the man ascribe it to his skill, That thorough grace has gained victory: If any strength we have, it is to ill, But all the good is Gods, both power and eke will. (II, x, i)

"And is there in heaven?" Spenser asks (II, viii, i), and adds:

.... But O! th' exceeding grace Of highest God that loves his creatures so And all his workes with mercy doth embrace...

Actually there are many different lands within "Faerie lond," but it is the affirmative, triumphant side of it that Spenser emphasizes emotionally. This "happy" land is not "th'aboundance of an ydle braine" (II, i, i). No, this is a fresh and vigorous region; it is like the exciting, newly discovered land of Peru, of the Amazon, of "fruitfullest Virginia." This is the realm of an idealized Queen Elizabeth herself:

And thou, O fayrest Princesse under sky! In this fayre mirrhour maist behold thy face, And thine owne realmes in lond of Faery, And in this antique ymage thy great auncestry.

Spenser has no difficulty in separating this "happy" land from the assortment of horrors also presented in the narrative:

The waies, through which my weary steps I guyde, In this delightfull land of Faery, Are so exceeding spacious and wyde, And sprinkled with such sweet variety Of all that pleasant is to eare or eye, That I, nigh ravisht with rare thoughts delight, My tedious travell doe forgo thereby; And when I gin to feele decay of might, It strength to me supplies, and cheers my dulled spright. (VI, i, i)

THE POETIC CONTRIBUTION

Modern taste in poetry differs radically from that of the Renaissance. We are used to short, incisive, imagistic statements, often highly personal and indicative of inner psychological tensions. We are also used to short, cryptic statements of hard-hitting social criticism. We have to make some sort of readjustment, therefore, to a long, leisurely, highly ornate narrative poem. It is like moving from the drastic architectural strength of Frank Lloyd Wright to the contorted forms and exaggerated pictorial effects of Bernini. Spenser wrote in a "baroque" tradition of masque, tableau, and allegorical "emblem." In the October Eclogue of *The Shepheardes Calender*, Spenser had said of poetry that it was "no arte, but a divine gift and heavenly instinct, not to bee gotten by laboure and learning, but adorned with both, and poured into the witte by a certain enthusiasm and celestial inspiration. . ." Spenser here follows a Renaissance derivation of Plato's thought in identifying the good with the beautiful, and regards the poet's function as using the world of the senses as a road to the unseen world of universal "essences" and "archetypes" (primal patterns). As a Christian, as well as a follower of Plato, he finds God reflected in the beauty of woman, but the world of the senses is always to leave the poet unsatisfied. The poet cannot rest in the beauty he sees, but must renounce it to pursue his "quest" (search, literally "hunt") This use of the world of the senses, of "images," to reach the spiritual world was a principle of Renaissance education and is embodied, in among other places, The Spiritual Exercise of St. Ignatius Loyola. Renaissance people were probably more gravely concerned with abstractions than we are, and they were less casual and glib in approaching them. To move from the concrete, visualized world to that of "pure" though had to be done in easy stages, and the mind had to be wooed and won.

Spenser thought of the poet as primarily as inspired teacher, particular concerned with moral instruction. He did not think, in the modern manner, that the artist's function was merely to express himself and his personal moods and thoughts, whatever they may be.

Spenser capitalized on the Renaissance effort to unite classical and Christian tradition; he even goes further and adds another ingredient, "the matter of Brittainy," the Arthurian legend and its derivatives. In painting one picture after another in the emblem tradition of the baroque, he draws on practically every source. His **imagery** can be very natural or very literary, or a combination of the two. Some images, like Belphoebe herself, are of "the womb of morning dew" and their "conception of the joyous prime." Here Irena is compared to a rose, when she knows that Sir Artegall will be her champion:

Like as a tender rose in open plaine, That with untimely drought nigh withered was, And hung the head, soone as few drops of raine Thereon distill, and deaw her daintie face, Gins to looke up, and with fresh wonted grace Dispreds the glorie of her leaves gay... (V, xii, xiii

Some are natural to the point straightforward **realism**. Here is a simile for a knight being set upon and pinned down:

As when a sturdy ploughman with his hynd By strength have overthrowne a stubborne steare They down him hold and fast with cords to bynde Till they him force the buxome yoke to beare. . (VI, vii, xi

Here is a highly literary image, used in reference to the mortal battle between the Red Cross Knight and his "Sarazin" foe, involving a griffin and a dragon:

So th'one for wrong, the other strives for right. As when a Gryfon, seized of his pray, A Dragon fierce encountreth in his flight, Through widest ayre making his ydle way, That would his rightful ravine rend away... (I, v, viii)

Spenser is very fond of sea-images, Here he presents a basically simple, universal image but steeped in literary allusion:

Much like, as when the beaten marinere, That long hath wandred in the Ocean wide, Oft soust in swelling Tethys saltish teare; And long time having tand his tawny hide With blustring breath of Heaven, that none can bide, And scorching flames of fierce Orions hound; Soone as the port from far he has espide, His chearfull whistle merily doth sound, And Nereus crownes with cups; his mates him pledg around. (I, iii, xxxi)

This last image is an example of the "Homeric" **simile** which Spenser constantly employs, Where in an ordinary **simile**, a writer says A is like B, in a Homeric **simile**, A is compared to B, but then a complete picture of B is presented with many graphic details not essential to the actual comparison but of interest in themselves.

Though the **imagery** of *The Faerie Queene* is of many different kinds, the repeated pattern or motif is that of the armed knight on horseback going through the tall forest (by no means Northern woods - we even have palm trees) intercepted by sunlight, shadow, spring and restful glade:

Covered with mossie shrubs, which spredding brode Did underneath them make a gloomy shade: Where foot of living creature never trode... (V, iv, xiii)

While Spenser is easily melodious, he seldom allows lyricism to outrun the demands of narrative structure. His skilled onomatopeia (the device whereby the sound accentuates the sense of words) is seldom overdone:

And more to lulle him in his slumber soft, A trickling streame from high rock tumbling downe, And ever-drizling raine upon the loft, Mixt with a murmuring winde, much like the sowne Of swarming Bees, did cast him in a swowne. No other noyse, nor people's troublous cryes, As still are wont t'annoy the walled towne, Might there be heard; but careless Quiet lyes Wrapt in eternall silence farre from enimyes. (I, i, xii)

The nine-line Spenserian stanze (rhyming ababbcbcc), consisting of nine iambic **pentameter** lines, with the exception of the last line, which is known as an "Alexandrine" of six iambic feet, creates a special musical effect, very suitable to its subject matter. John Milton thinks of the general theme of *The Faerie Queene* when he lists his reading in Il Penseroso:

And if aught else great Bards beside In sage and solemn tunes have sung, Of Tourneys and of Trophies hung, Of Forests, and enchantments drear, Where more is meant than meets the ear.

But in L'Allegro, he is thinking of the Spenserian **stanza** itself, with its carefully inter-linked rhymes, and the lengthening out of the final effect in the Alexandrine:

Lap me in soft Lydian Airs Married to immortal verse, Such as the meeting soul may pierce In notes, with many a winding bout Of linked sweetness long drawn out, With wanton heed, and giddy cunning, The melting voice through mazes running...

Meaning, more than meets the ear, is expressed in linked sweetness long drawn out. The actual effect of the final line of the Spenserian **stanza** is to give a sense of pause at the end, as if the reader had journeyed forward a pace and now had time to stop and look around. Obviously *The Faerie Queene* was never designed for a quick reading. It is to be taken in sections, slowly and fully.

THE LANGUAGE OF THE FAERIE QUEENE

While the language of *The Faerie Queene* may present difficulties to the modern reader, they are of a minor range of difficulty, compared, let us say with *The Shephearde's Calender*.

First is the matter of spelling. After some acquaintance with this, one develops a knack for seeing the equivalent modern word. Words like "arownd," "confownd," (w for ou) look odd enough at first, but create no trouble. The same holds of past participles formed with Y as in "ykindled" and "ydrad." More puzzling are the addition or omission of "e's". Most "e's" at the end of words are not pronounced (thus "ayre" is modern "air") In the interior of words, "e's" are pronounced in Spenserian spelling or else they are omitted, being marked with the sign of elision (the apostrophe). In modern English we print "e's" even when we don't pronounce them. Thus the word "difference" is today pronounced with two syllables. Spenser if he had pronounced it as we do would have spelled it "diff'rence." In the following Spenserian line, "difference" is pronounced dif-fe-rence.

And waters fall with difference discreet

As for the meaning of words, even when there is trouble, the reader after a while finds the right meaning from the context. A mounting difficulty occurs when the word is now obsolete, or now used in a different sense. "Spright" is not easily recognizable as "spirit." A word like "eke" meaning "also" may have to be found in a glossary, attached to most editions.

An ear for the meter will sometimes indicate the need to pronounce an extra syllable, different from modern practice:

That thorough grace has gained victory (Through - two syllables; gained - two syllables) Are so exceeding spacious and wide (Spacious - three syllables, spa-ci-ous)

Spenser's language was criticized in his own era. Ben Jonson said that Spenser, in "affecting" the ancients, "writ no language." There is this much truth in this stringent criticism: Spenser was formulating a special style of vocabulary for his work. Tasso had argued in Discourses on Heroic Poetry that uncommon words, and words from antiquity and other languages, could be used, provided they were sufficiently recognizable. Spenser was an enthusiast about Chaucer; he is "Dan Chaucer, well of English undefyld" (Faerie Queene, IV, ii, xxxii). He is

That old Dan Geffrey (in whose gentle spright, The pure well head of poesie did dwell) (VII, vii, ix)

In so far as Spenser has a special type of vocabulary, it is largely reminiscent of Chaucer.

But Spenser does use words that never became part of the language: giambeaux (leggings), amenaunce (carriage, behavior), surquedry (pride, insolence), souvenaunce (remembrance). "Taking conge" (taking leave), which Spenser uses frequently, has remained with us, though never really assimilated into the language. Describing so many battles between knights as he does, Spenser uses a number of technical terms of combat: haberjeon (armor for neck and breast), burganet (helmet), pannikel (skull), hauberk (coat of mail). Words from Anglo-Saxon, as distinct from Romance, sources, include ympe (the shoot of a tree - hence, a young man), lozell (a worthless fellow), awhape (to terrify), and the nearly all-purpose word, dight (to deal with, to do, to compose, to put on, to dress, prepare, make ready).

THE FAERIE QUEENE

TEXTUAL ANALYSIS

BOOK I

GENERAL THEME

In Spenser's own words, the first book contains "the legend" of the Knight of the Red Cross, or of Holiness." The word "legend" comes from a Latin word meaning "something that should be read." In actual practice, the word "legend: is applied to a traditional "creative" story (often with some reference to history, and even actually presented as authentic history). The legend, according to medieval custom, often developed moral and allegorical significance (see introduction).

The two principal characters in Book I are the Red Cross Knight, representing Truth, and Una, "pure and innocent as a lamb" (the lamb being a symbol of Christ), representing divine revealed truth. While Spenser adapts Aristotle's definitions of the various virtues, and the distinctions between them, he by no means accepts Aristotle without very important modifications. The idea of holiness, for example, comes specifically from Judaic-Christian sources, particularly in its medieval applications. Holiness means "oneness" in the sense that a virtuous man exercises justice in every department of life. He is consistent and, allowing for occasional weaknesses, unfluctuating. Virtue for Spenser, who follows Plato in this respect (as in the dialogue in the Protagoras) is not the sum total of the different virtues. Rather virtue is one and entire, just as parts of the face form the whole face. The names of particular virtues (like parts of the face) follow from applying the common basis of virtue to the differing particulars of life. Thus patriotism might be defined through the common basis of justice as "justice" towards one's country, "love" as justice towards one's friend or one's mate - in the words of the seventeenth century poem, "I could not love thee, dear, so much, Loved I not honor more." The basic unity of all the virtues is paralleled by Spenser in calling the symbol of truth Una (a Latin feminine adjective meaning "one.")

So far, so good. But Spenser combines with this Platonic concept of virtue as "oneness" and unity the Christian idea of Divine Grace. From Plato (and Aristotle) comes the idea of the complete man, with integrity or oneness, possessing all the natural virtues. But for Spenser this would not in itself constitute holiness. Spenser's view is partly the result of the fact that the pagan virtues, as understood both by Plato and Aristotle, do not completely square with the medieval system. Humility, for example is specifically a Christian virtue - one which, as we shall see, the Red Cross Knight has to struggle to learn. This is supernatural virtue, that is, one above nature, the result of Grace, outside the Aristotelian system.

In keeping with the conditions of the allegory in Book I, the Red Cross Knight is a pilgrim to eternity (in Canto X, he has a vision of the Heavenly Jerusalem, but he has a lot to work to do before he can reach it). He represents the "Church militant" - that is to say, he is a Christian in a state of conflict, development, "becoming," fighting his own recurrent weaknesses as well as injustice in the world at large. He has to go back, as it were, for special retraining programs, involving study, reflection, penances, as in the House of Holiness (Canto X). He has to learn and develop a great deal, before he tackles the dragon of iniquity in the last Canto.

Una is not presented, as the Red Cross Knight is, in terms of conflict and development. She is divine truth, constant and unchanging. She is of "heavenly" birth, that is - of "revealed" religious truth. She is "veiled" as a sign of her almost frightening brilliance (similar to the way "Contemplation" is clad in black in Milton's Il Penseroso). She must wear this veil because, except under special conditions, mankind could not at once bear the "brightness" of her divine truth. Natural reason is symbolized by her attendant dwarf - he is so far surpassed in stature by revealed truth. Since Una is unchanging, knowing no "mutability" (a favorite Spenserian word), she is not involved in the world of action (and, therefore, of some frustration and defeat). The Red Cross Knight, on the other hand, is applying truth in a world of opposition and misunderstanding (including his own inner problems). Una is truth, a source of spiritual strength to the Knight, but is unable in her allegorical function to give him direct aid. In the final climactic struggle with the dragon, she has to stand to one side, a concerned but passive spectator.

One of the things that has to be kept in mind in the reading of Spenser is the fact that, though he is a good story-teller, his characters do not always behave as human beings might be expected to behave. Una does not always behave as a woman. As a woman, she might have thought of some means of helping the Red Cross Knight in his struggle with the dragon. But, as allegorical dispassionate truth, in a kind of abstract sense, she has to keep apart. If Spenser's figures do not always behave like human beings, after the reader has been led to expect that they would, the reason is to be found in the nature of the allegory itself. If noting this, one should also keep in mind that not everything which raises a question in the reader's mind will be answered by the working of the allegory. Not all the details, not all the things that happen in *The Faerie Queene* are meant to be allegorical.

A note should be added here, at the beginning of the reading of *The Faerie Queene*, for readers not totally familiar with medieval terms. We must not think of England as a densely populated country as it is today. It is estimated that in Elizabeth's time, the total population was under three millions. "Nature" could still be dangerous, and the "laws" of hospitality, influenced by religion, were very strict, particularly in rural areas. Malbecco (Book III, ix) and Briana (IV, i) violate these rules and are open to punishment. Briana abuses the "custom" of the castle. A host could not "charge" the stranger who availed himself of his hospitality, but the stranger was expected to express his gratitude by some service or other (the "custom"). In the case of Briana, the custom insisted upon is degrading to the guest, and could therefore be refused.

The term "squire" is frequently met. A squire was a probationer for knighthood. After proving himself in military experience and demonstrating honorable conduct, he could be made a knight. The term comes from a French word, escuyer, meaning a "shield-bearer."

DETAILED SUMMARY AND ANALYSIS OF BOOK I

Canto I

The Red Cross Knight, with a silver shield battered and dented as a result of many conflicts, with a cross on his breast the color of blood, has set out, on the orders of the Glorious Queen of Faerie to destroy a dragon, "horrible and stern." A lovely lady, her face concealed by a veil, rides beside him. The lady is descended of a royal line whose scepters have governed shores from east to west. She leads by a cord a milk-white lamb. Trailing behind her is a dwarf carrying her baggage. (Christ came into Jerusalem riding upon a donkey, preparatory to his Passion. The lamb is the Paschal Lamb, a symbol of a sacrifice important both in Judaism and Christianity.).

A storm breaks, and this curious group has to seek shelter under lofty trees bearing leaves so broad that light scarcely enters the forest. At last they come to a hollow cave amid the thickest woods. The lady warns her companion that they have come to the "wandering wood, foul error's Den." And the dwarf (natural reason) points out that this is no place for living men.

But the Red Cross Knight plunges in, his glistening armor making a little light in the dark hole. There he comes face to face with a repulsive monster, half serpent, half woman (a combination of the deceived Eve and of the deceiver, the Father of Lies, in Genesis). The monster is prolific, with a thousand young ones feeding on her poisonous. dugs. It hates light, particularly the spiritual light of truth. A terrific battle takes place. She wraps herself around the Knight, and he cannot stir hand or foot. The lady cries out warning the Knight that either he strangle Error or be strangled by her! The Knight manages to kill the monster, and from her corpse comes a vomit full of books and papers. Her offspring crowd around the dying mother and suck her blood.

The group continues its journey and comes upon an old man dressed all in black, sad in appearance, saying his prayers as he walks. He claims to know nothing of the world from which he has retired to live in his forest cell. But he does know of a strange man who ravages the surrounding countryside. They arrive at the old man's hermitage, and the "holy" man (actually the evil enchanter, Archimago, presumably symbolic of Spain and the Catholic Church) intersperses his talk of saints and popes with prayers. When his guests are asleep, he casts spells upon them, taken out of his books of black magic.

Calling upon Great Gorgon, prince of darkness and dead night. At which Cocytus quakes, and Styx is put to flight he finds two spirits summoned from the lower world suitable for his work. One is sent to the House of Morpheus (god of sleep) with a request that the Red Cross Knight be subjected to a special erotic dream. The other spirit is made to represent a beautiful woman the double of the Una herself. The Red Cross Knight dreams that his own Una is offering herself dishonorably to him.

Canto II

When he is awake, the Red Cross Knight is led to think that he has seen Una committing sin with an unknown stranger, a young squire. The knight and the dwarf leave in disgust. The true, innocent Una, the victim of Archimago's deceits, is left abandoned and unprotected to roam the forests.

Meanwhile the Red Cross Knight meets a Saracen, Sansfoy ("without Faith"), accompanied by an immoral woman clad in red scarlet (symbol of sin as in the Book of Revelation), wearing a Persian mitre. She encourages her lover to attack the Red Cross Knight, and the Red Cross knight kills him.

He pities this woman, Fidessa, who has apparently lost her lover. According to her account, she, the sole daughter of an emperor, had been betrothed to a handsome prince, who had been slain by his foes before the wedding day. Sansfoy had then abducted her, she asserts, but their relationship had been without dishonor.

Continuing his journey Fidessa, the Red Cross Knight seeks to rest under the shades of two enormous trees. He plucks a bough from one of them to make a garland for Fidessa's head. But as the branch breaks, some drops of blood exude from a rift in the wood, and a voice begs him not to tear the flesh of the man imprisoned in the tree, nor that of the wretched lady held fast in the neighboring tree! One tree had once been Fradubio; the other, his beloved Fraelissa. Fradubio had killed Duessa's companion who had boasted that his lady (Duessa) was more beautiful than Fraelissa. Duessa had then yielded herself prisoner to Fradubio. Fradubio had been tactless enough one day to determine who was more beautiful, Fraelissa or Duessa. Duessa won the contest through trickery, and Fraelissa was left behind, converted to a tree. Fradubio had enjoyed Duessa for his "dame" until a certain day when he found out that she really was a witch, foul, old, and ugly - whereupon Duessa meted out the same treatment to Fradubio she had to Fraelissa.

Canto III

Meanwhile Una, afraid of nothing, seeks her knight in wildernesses and deserts. While resting one day in a shady place, she is about to be attacked by a savage lion. But when the lion comes near to her, he behaves quite differently. He kisses her feet, licks her hands; innocence and beauty tame him. Una weeps, comparing the lion's gentle behavior to that of the other lion, the Red Cross Knight. Mounting her horse again, she finds the lion following her, proud to guard her.

She meets a woman carrying a pot of water. The woman runs home, where her mother "blind, sat in eternal night." Una arrives at the cottage where Corceca (blink devotionalism) prays in a corner, devoutly penitent. Kirkrapine (church plunderer) brings stolen goods to her daughter, Abessa, with whom he has immoral relations. The lion rends him into a thousand pieces.

The old woman and her daughter run cursing after Una when she leaves. In the meantime Archimago has disguised himself as the Red Cross Knight. He overtakes Una, who now mistakes him for her true knight; she is happy and reconciled. Archimago continues to play his cruel, deceitful game. They encounter Sansloy ("without law"). Sansloy attacks Archimago, in the belief that he is the true Red Cross Knight who had killed his brother Sansfoy He knocks Archimago from his horse and is about to kill him. Una pleads, but Sansloy, unpitying and relentless, lifts the helmet of his fallen opponent-only discover that he is indeed Archimago! - - - whereupon Sansloy seizes Una, but is attached by the lion. The brave lion dies under the spear of the terrifying Sansloy, and Una is left for a moment at the mercy of his rage and lust.

Canto IV

In the meantime the authentic Red Cross Knight has been traveling with Duessa, believing that she is really Fidessa. They come to the mansion of a mighty prince. High walls hung with golden foil, delightful bowers, and galleries make it impressive. Yet it was built on sand and every breath of heaven shook it! It outside was sumptuous, excelling ancient Persia with its pompous pride. Enthroned against of cloth of state was a maiden queen shining like the sun, and underneath her feet was a dreadful dragon with a hideous train. Lucifera (the Latin feminine for Lucifer, prince of devils), was the daughter of Pluto and Porserpina, the rulers of Hell. Lucifera followed no rule of law in her realm, but, rather, simple expediency under the advice of six wizards whose names speak for themselves. They were Idleness, dressed in black like a monk; Gluttony, who bore a "bouzing can" in his hands; Lechery, riding a bearded goat; Avarice, carrying two iron coffers; Envy, upon a ravenous wolf, in his teeth a venomous toad, in his bosom a snake; Wrath, upon a lion, his clothes stained with blood. Behind them comes Satan with a "smarting" whip in his hand. Sansjoy ("without joy") sees the Red Cross Knight and challenges him to fight. Duessa is worried.

Canto V

On the next day Lucifera, under a stately canopy, watches the fight. In the course of a fierce battle when Sansjoy is about to lose, he is covered with a thick mist. The Red Cross Knight is honored as the victor of the Field. Duessa, apparently weeping over the wounds of the Red Cross Knight, plays a double game as usual. She appeals to dreaded Night, most "ancient grandmother of all" to rescue Sansjoy, but even Night cannot turn back the stream of destiny, or break the chains of Necessity. But Duessa revealing to Night who she truly is, the daughter of deceit and shame, persuandes Night to take the body of Sansjoy into her chariot and convey it to hell, the sights of which are then described in traditional mythological terms. Sansjoy is restored to life by Aesculapius, the "father" of medicine.

Meanwhile, in a dungeon the Red Cross Knight has seen huge numbers of wretches who had mortgaged their lives to covetousness. He decides to leave the unwholesome place quickly and, in the dawning light as he sets out, he sees a dunghill of carcasses, "the dreadful spectacle of that sad house of pride." He is still unaware that Fidessa is really Duessa in disguise.

Canto VI

We now return to Una, who had been left alone with the fierce Sansloy. He immediately makes every effort to seduce her, but she remains as steadfast as a "rock of diamond." She is rescued in the nick of time by a troop of Fauns and Satyrs, wild wood gods, who managed to frighten Sansloy away from his intended wickedness. Glad as "birds of joyous prime," they sing around Una, and bring her Sylvanus (the chief god of the pastoral woods). She stays with the "savage" people a long time, teaching them the truth.

Satyrane, the son of a Satyr and a lady seduced by him, visits the woods where Una is living. Satyrane, known throughout the land of Faerie for his manhood and courage, has been brought up as a tough woodsman and hunter. He admires Una's heavenly grace and sacred lore, and helps her to escape from the Satyrs who worship her.

Leaving together, they encounter a traveler, with torn sandals, sun-tanned, walking with a stick (Archimago again!). He informs them that the Red Cross Knight is dead, the victim of paynim ("pagan") sword. Archimago is exploiting his own humiliation in Canto III when he fell disguised as the Red Cross Knight, before Sansloy. Satyrane comes upon the "miscreant," Sansloy, now wearing the armor of the Red Cross Knight, taken from Archimago. Sansloy denies killing the Red Cross Knight; he is simply wearing his arms. But Satyrane and Sansloy fight anyhow, while Una flees away.

Canto VII

Duessa discovers that the Red Cross Knight has fled from the House of Pride. She finds him disarmed by a fountain side, and reproaches him for having left her (she was then Fidessa, of course). The Red Cross Knight drinks of the spring at hand which had been enchanted so that whoever drank of it waxed "dull and slow." He is about to become an easy victim for Duessa's wiles when his "goodly court" of the lady is disturbed by a horrible sound coming from a hideous giant, born of Earth, and Aeolus, the blustering wind.

Though puffed up with empty wind, the giant has unlimited arrogance. He attacks the unharmed knight with a giant oak tree. Duessa pleads that Orgoglio (for so the giant was named) spare the Red Cross Knight. In return she will become Orgoglio's bondslave and "leman" (mistress). The Red Cross Knight is made a prisoner.

Orgoglio crowns Duessa with a triple crown (like the Papal crown), and gives her gold and purple to wear. He also gives her a filthy monster with seven heads, an iron breast, a back full of brassy scales, with bloody eyes shining like glass. Its enormous tail stretched to the heavens

And with extorted powre, and borrow'd strength, The everburning lamps from thence it brought...

Bearing its rider, Duessa, it treaded all sacred things beneath its feet.

The dwarf of the Red Cross Knight witnessed these events, and departed with his master's armor, spear, and shield. On the way he meets Una again, still in flight from the paynim Sansloy whom Satyrane engaged in battle. Seeing the equipment in the dwarf's possession, she immediately fears that the Red Cross Knight is dead. Her pitying heart "pants and quakes." She swoons and throws herself on the ground.

The dwarf gives her a summary of events to date: the subtle tricks of old Archimago, the wanton loves of false Fidessa, the wretched couple turned into trees, the House of Pride, the combat of the Red Cross Knight with Sansloy, the luckless combat with Orgoglio. Una at least feels better, knowing that the Red Cross Knight may still be alive.

They see a knight coming toward them, his glittering armor from head to toe shining far away, with a belt of precious stones (one stone blazing like Hesperus among the other stars was shaped like a lady's head). His sword was sheathed in ivory and had a hilt of burnished gold. His helmet bore the crest of a dragon with golden wings. He carried a shield made of pure diamond, kept covered because its blazing light turned men into stone-a protective and defensive weapon immune to the enchanter's art (a good insurance for the goings-on in *The Faerie Queene!*). The great enchanter Merlin had himself made the shield and sword, the armor for Prince Arthur himself whom we now meet for the first time. Tactfully he draws out from Una the secret of her troubles. He assures her that she has cause to complain (Surely an understatement!). He promises that he will not leave her until he has rescued the Red Cross Knight from Orgoglio.

Canto VIII

Arthur's squire, Timias, blows a tremendous horn before the castle of Orgoglio, where the Red Cross Knight is imprisoned. The castle seems deserted, its gates shut. But, with the piercing note of the horn, everything bursts open. The giant puts aside at once his "dalliance" (cf. the word "dilly-dally") with Duessa to find out what **catastrophe** is impending. She follows Orgoglio on her impressive seven-headed monster.

A tremendous battle ensues between Orgoglio and the Red Cross Knight. Orgoglio uses heavy equipment-a dreadful club, "all arm'd with ragged snubbes and knottie graine," but he lacks marksmanship. With a clever thrust, the knight smites off Orgoglio's left arm, which falls like a block to the ground, the blood flowing like a river from a rock. Duessa at this point brings in her dreadful beast as a reserve, but the squire heads him off. Duessa then sprinkles upon Timias an enchanted poison that makes him useless as a fighter. Arthur lops off one of the accessory heads of the monster, but things are going well, for he has to fight both the monster and Orgoglio! Finally he uncovers his diamond shield. Apparently it would have been unsporting, though certainly practical, for Arthur to have used this at first! But, since Duessa broke the laws of chivalry as they pertained to single combat, Arthur is now justified in its use. Duessa is temporarily blinded. Arthur brings the giant down to size by smiting off his right leg at the knee, and follows up with a truly decisive gesture - by beheading him! The squire makes the "scarlet whore" his prisoner.

They enter the castle. Ignaro ("ignorance") answers their questions about the whereabouts of the Red Cross Knight by constantly repeating "he could not tell." The castle is richly decorated with gold and tapestry, but the floor is covered with the blood of guiltless babes. They find the Red Cross Knight feeble, with eyes dull in their hollow pits, arms rawbone.

Duessa is stripped naked of her royal purple robes. She looks perfectly horrible-her bald head being only a minor feature of her repulsive person. For such is the face of falsehood. In the meantime the rescued and the rescuers rest at the castle.

Canto IX

Spenser tells us of the background and ancestry of Arthur. At birth he was given to the charge of a faery knight, old Timon, to be brought up as a gentleman and as a knight. Timon, living under Mount Rauran by the river Dee in Wales, was expert in all martial skills. Merlin visited Arthur and supervised his development. Merlin kept the names of Arthur's parents secret from him, though he did say Arthur was the son and heir of a king, and at the right time he would learn who he was. But as we see him now, Arthur is suffering from a grievous, internal wound, for he is in love! Timon has warned him to keep such inclinations under the control of reason. Arthur has had a vision of his love, the Queen of Faeries, in a dream. The Red Cross Knight assures him that he lady, whom Arthur has not yet seen, is the most beautiful of virgins, "full of heavenly light, of wondrous faith, exceeding earthly grace." After an exchange of gifts, Arthur goes on his way to seek his love; the Red Cross Knight resumes his journey to fight the dragon, Una's foe.

The Red Cross Knight, accompanied by Una, is not yet fully recovered from the effects of his imprisonment. He meets the armed Sir Trevisan, minus his helmet, running in a hysterical state, pale, with his hair standing on end. Around his neck is a hempen rope. Sir Trevisan stops to tell his story of how he had been traveling with Sir Terwin, who had been in love with a woman contemptuous of his passion. Together they had met a man of hell named Despair. Despair had persuaded Sir Terwin to kill himself.

The travelers, with the exception of Sir Trevisan who refuses to approach the place, reach the darksome cave of Despair, where they see the body of Sir Terwin wallowing in luke-warm blood. Despair, far from being dismayed, argues with persuasive psychology that the Red Cross Knight should also kill himself.

Sleepe after toyle, port after stormie seas, Ease after warre, death after life, does greatly please.

Despair argues that necessity itself decides the date of men's death, and, therefore, suicide itself is determined within the laws of necessity. He even goes so far as to persuade the knight, who is in a weakened condition anyhow, that he is already damned because of the failings of his past life. Despair actually puts a dagger in the hands of the Red Cross Knight, and the latter's hands tremble! Una, in cold fright, snatches it away from him, reminding him of a more constructive assignment-fighting the fire-mouthed dragon, horrible and bright. She reminds the knight of the realities of mercy and justice. Despair, failing to destroy the Red Cross Knight, hangs himself with a halter! Yet he cannot die!

Canto X

Spenser says that no man should ascribe victory over spiritual foes to his own skill, but rather to divine grace. Aware that the Red Cross Knight is still weak, Una brings him to recover his strength at the House of Holiness, renowned throughout the world for "sacred lore and pure unspotted life," under the direction of a grave matron, named Dame Caelia. Caelia has two unmarried daughters, Fidelia and Speranza, and one married, Charissa.

The travelers are admitted by a porter named Humilita, and are greeted by Zeal and Reverence. Caelia welcomes Una as "most virtuous virgin, born of heavenly birth." She is pleasantly surprised that Una and her knight are visiting the house:

…………So few there bee, That chose the narrow path, or seeke the right.

Fidelia bears a cup of gold filled to the brim with wine and water, in which a serpent lies enfolded, and a book signed and sealed with blood, wherein hidden things, hard to understand, are written. Speranza, dressed in blue, the color of modesty, bears a silver anchor on her arm. After introductions to Faith and Hope (Fidelia, Speranza), the guests are led by Obedience to an appropriate lodging.

Fidelia teaches the Red Cross Knight celestial discipline out of her mysterious book, stressing the meaning of God, grace, justice, and free will. The lessons take so well that the Red Cross Knight begins to "abhore" the wretched world. At this point Speranza takes over his schooling, to bring him to a better spiritual balance. He has to learn to take sure hold of her silver anchor, else concentration on his past sins will cause him to lose the main points of Fidelia's teaching.

Others help him, too. Patience doctors him, prescribing sackcloth and ashes; Penance provides him with an iron whip. But, above all, Charissa ("Charity" - "the greatest of all these is Charity"), with turtle doves on an ivory chain as symbols of happy married love, instructs in the Christian idea of love. She had not previously met the Red Cross Knight because she had been giving birth to a child. Charity leads him to Mercy, who guides him to a hospital where various human ills and miseries are tended.

After the Red Cross Knight has performed various good works, he visits a hermitage nearby, where lives an aged holy man named Contemplation. Contemplation's physical eyesight is poor for he is very old indeed; embodying youthful spiritually, he has keen spiritual sight:

For God he often saw from heavens height...

The old man, at the request of Mercy, guides the Red Cross Knight to the highest mount, like that of Moses or that on which Christ gave his famous sermon. The Red Cross Knight views a great city built high of pearls and precious stone, indescribable by man, where dwell eternal peace and happiness. This is the New Jerusalem that God built for his chosen people, a city excelling in beauty even Cleopolis, the seat of the Faerie Queen herself. The old man predicts that the Red Cross Knight will be among those "eternized" in the "immortal book of fame," and that he shall be known as "Saint George of Mery England."

The Red Cross Knight does not want to return to the world. The old man, however, reveals to him the secret of his parentage. The Red Cross Knight springs from an ancient race of Saxon kings. He had been a changeling, stolen by a faerie from his human parents who were left a faery child in his place. A ploughman found the child and gave him the name George.

Returning to Una from the mountain, the Red Cross Knight finds that his eyes have been dazed by the brightness of the vision.

Canto XI

Now we come to the great battle between the Red Cross Knight and the old dragon. Una's parents have imprisoned themselves in a tower of brass to escape the terror which the knight is now to meet. A horrible roaring which shakes the ground is heard; then the dragon is seen stretched along the sunny side of great hill, himself a great hill! Making a terrific shadow, the dragon, horrible and vast, approaches our courageous St. George.

Plated with scales, the monster has wings like two great sails with which he can move with unexpected speed through the terrified sky. His tail has a hundred folds with thick entangled knots, red and black, stretching little short of three furlongs. It is needless to mention his claws and devouring teeth. His still bloody teeth are iron. In addition, he gives forth smothering smoke and sulfur.

The Red Cross Knight drives his pointed steel at him, as can be imagined, with little effect. The dragon retaliates by picking up both man and horse and driving them through the air. When the monster is forced to come down for a moment and let go of his victims, the Red Cross Knight drives his spear, using the strength of three men, into the dragon's body close under the left wing. Black blood, the force of which could drive a watermill, gushes forth and drowns the land. The dragon replies with fire, burning the knight's armor and singeing his body underneath. The Red Cross Knight has the worst of it, what with "heat, toil, wounds, arms, smart, inward fire."

The dragon knocks the knight into a well. Fortunately, this is the "well of life" possessing medicinal properties, which can restore the dead to life. The dragon claps his wings, feeling very pleased with himself. Una spends the first night of the battle in prayer.

But in the morning the Red Cross Knight comes out of the well, like an eagle, fresh as the morning wave. This time the Red

Cross Knight starts operations by striking a yawning wound into the crested scalp of his enemy, and the latter roars like a hundred rampaging lions. The dragon shoots his sting, like a needle, through the knight's armor, where it breaks off and remains painfully embedded. Enraged with pain, the Red Cross Knight cleaves the dragon's tail down to the stump. Finally, the knight cuts off the dragon's feet which had clutched his shield and which still cling remorselessly after they have been cut off. The dragon then uses his smoke and flame-throwers, and the Red Cross Knight goes down for the count.

Again the Red Cross Knight is fortunate. He falls beside a tree, loaded with vermillion apples, called the Tree of Life. This tree gave a sovereign balm that could cure mortal wounds. Night falls, and Una prays and waits.

The third phase of the battle is the last. The dragon tries to swallow the Red Cross Knight whole, but the Knight, taking advantage of the open mouth, thrusts his sword through it to the dragon's stomach, and down falls the monster like a huge cliff.

Canto XII

The watchman from the castle wall sees the dead monster. The aged sire, lord of the land, opens the castle gate. The Red Cross Knight is greeted by the King and Queen; dancing virgins throw laurel boughs before him; Una is crowned with a green garland. The crowd approaches the dead monster cautiously, afraid that somewhere near him may be a nest of small dragons.

The floor of the castle is spread with the royal purple of welcome. The Knight is proclaimed the King's heir and the future husband of his daughter, Una:

So faire and fresh, as freshest flowre in May, For she had layd her mournefull stole aside, And widow-like sad wimple throwne away Wherewith her heavenly beautie she did hide Whiles on her wearie journey she did ride...

All stand in amazement of Una's revealed beauty.

Then a stranger arrives with a message, apparently from Fidessa but in reality from Duessa, stating that the Knight had already plighted his hand to another love in another country. But the Knight identifies Fidessa as Duessa, and Una fingers the messenger as Archimago. Archimago is arrested and thrown into a dungeon. Una and the Red Cross Knight are finally married:

Great joy was made that day of young and old, And solemne feast proclatmd throughout the land, That their exceeding merth may not be told...

But the Red Cross Knight shortly had to leave Una, and report back the success of his exploit to the Faerie Queen.

THE FAERIE QUEENE

TEXTUAL ANALYSIS

BOOK II

GENERAL THEME

The **theme** of Book II is that of Temperance, the great natural virtue of self-control which checks passion and the tendency to go to extremes. This is the basic virtue that underlies the Aristotelian system; in the words of Pauline Parker, "the ability to act, as virtue requires, because all the natural powers and qualities are held in due subjection, so that they all work harmoniously together, and none assumes an irrational domination, is that virtue of exquisite balance which ancient Greek educational theory aimed at, and which Aristotle summarized in his doctrine of the mean." John Milton singles out this book for special comment in the "Areopagitica." Spenser does not prize a fugitive and cloistered virtue; rather Spenser "describing true temperance under the person of Guyon, brings him in with his palmer through the cave of Mammon and the bower of earthly bliss, that he might see and know, and yet abstain."

Spenser is careful to add a Christian safeguard to the idea of Temperance. Holiness, as in the case of the Red Cross Knight, can achieve its quest finally on its own. But Guyon is constantly guided by the palmer, representing reason and right judgment, allied to grace (for the palmer is a holy man). Temperance is not for Spenser a self-sufficient virtue as in pagan humanism.

Guyon is sometimes the victim of foolish pity (his sentimental sparing of Pyrochles in Canto V, his listening to the maid in misfortune in Canto XII). Only a resolute will can maintain true judgment, and Sir Guyon has to go through an educative process before he achieves his quest.

DETAILED SUMMARY AND ANALYSIS OF BOOK II

Canto I

Archimago, though he had been confined to a dungeon by Una's father, has managed to escape. Once more he tries to injure the Red Cross Knight, either by "forged reason or open fight," in spite of the Knight's recent outstanding victory over the dragon. Pretending to be a poor, nondescript squire, he tells Sir Guyon and his faithful palmer that the honor of a virgin has been violently attacked by a Knight. The palmer is technically a pilgrim who has returned from the Holy Land. He bears a staff in the story, representing the power of wisdom. Archimago leads them to the distraught lady. She (Duessa again in disguise!) identifies her attacker as the Red Cross Knight.

Sir Guyon attacks the Red Cross Knight, but even while charging against him, Sir Guyon recognizes his opponent's shield, the badge of the Redeemer's death. In turn, the Red Cross Knight identifies the "image of the heavenly maid" borne by Sir

Guyon. By an act of temperance and judgment Sir Guyon avoids, just in the nick of time, what might have been a tragic situation.

This trick of Archimago having failed, the black-clad palmer continues to guide Sir Guyon: Still him guided over dale and hill And with his steedy staffe did point the way, His race with reason, and with words his will From fowle intemperaunce he ofte did stay...

They hear a woman shrieking, calling for death. She is crying bitterly over her baby whose little hands are covered with blood stemming from her breast, in which a cruel knife is stuck. Sir Guyon removes the knife, helping her to regain consciousness. She tells how her husband, Sir Mortdant, seeking adventure, had fallen into the hands of Acrasia, the false enchantress, who lives in the Bower of Bliss on a wandering island in a "perilous" gulf. She had succeeded in making Sir Mortdant her lover, and Acrasia makes her lovers "drunken mad" (insane). After his wife had found him, she set out to restore him to health. But Acrasia gave him a charmed cup from which he drank, and he dropped down dead. She now dies beside the body of her husband. Sir Guyon and the Palmer bury them. Sir Guyon swears to take vengeance on behalf of the orphan child who has now fallen into his hands.

Canto II

Sir Guyon finds that he cannot clean the blood from the baby's hands, although he has bathed them in a sacred well, chaste and pure as the purest snow. The palmer says that the bloody hands are meant to remain as a sacred symbol of the mother's innocence. Sir Guyon, taking the baby in his hands, now finds his "lofty steed" missing. Carrying his little burden with him as he travels on foot, Sir Guyon comes to a castle built on a rock, adjoining the sea.

The ownership of the castle has been divided among three sisters, and two of them quarrel constantly. Medina, the "middle" sister, welcomes Guyon courteously and modestly. In the meantime the two other sisters are entertaining two suitors of "peerless puissance" (unequalled valor). Sir Huddibras courts the eldest, Elissa; Sansloy, who had attempted to dishonor Una in Book I, courts the youngest, Perissa. Both the sisters and their suitors resent the new arrival and want to battle him, but, before they can do this, they have a violent quarrel among themselves. Sir Guyon tries to intercede in the armed conflict between Huddibras and Sansloy, whereupon both fall upon him. Medina pleads in the name of the laws of knighthood and of love that they all desist:

Sad be the sights, and bitter fruites of warre, And thousand furies wait on wrathful sword...

Her eloquence restores "lovely concord and most sacred peace."

But the two sisters do not cooperate for long. Elissa, the eldest, was so discontented and melancholy that she would not eat. Perissa, the youngest, was "full of disport" and "loosely light." Sansloy equalled her in abandonment, while Huddibras was a "malcontent" suited to Elissa. And betwixt them both.

............the faire Medina sate With sober grace and goodly carriage.

Sir Guyon sees in Medina the image of the most glorious virgin queen alive who

In widest ocean she her throne does reare That over all the earth it may be seene...

Sir Guyon belongs to her "Order of Maidenhead."

Canto III

Sir Guyon commits the "bloody-handed" babe to the care of Medina who is to rear and educate him; he is given the name of Ruddymane ("Red hand").

A comic figure, a "losell" or a good-for-nothing, had taken the Knight's horse, spear, and shield. This Braggadocchio ("windy boasting") reminds one of a peacock in his painted plumes. He threatens a simple fellow seated on a sunny bank. In high-flown and threatening language he demands that this fellow yield himself his "vassal." This man, named Trompart, suitably kisses Braggadocchio's stirrup, but he is not such a fool as he looks. He thinks secretly that he can put Braggadocchio to his own use and exploit him.

This strange pair run into Archimago who ask them to avenge the slaying of Sir Mortdant, whose death Archimago attributes to Sir Guyon and the Red Cross Knight. Braggadocchio has no sword (for the Red Cross Knight had been using it when Braggadocchio stole the rest of his equipment). But he is such a boaster and has such unfounded confidence in himself that he will undertake to battle these knights without it:

Is not enough fowre quarters of a man, Withouten sword or shield, an hoste to quayle? Thou litle wotest what this right hand can.

THE FAERIE QUEENE AND OTHER WORKS

He is not going to use any sword, unless it is that of Prince Arthur himself, whereupon Archimago promises to get it. Archimago disappears into the air, leaving Braggadocchio and Trompart wondering!

Moving on, they hear a shrill hunting horn echoing through the woods. Braggadocchio dismounts and hides in the bushes. Finally, Trompart sees coming towards him "a goodly lady clad in hunter's weed" (costume). Her cheeks are like "roses in a bed of lilies shed." Her face is so beautiful that it could heal the sick and revive the dead. How Spenser asks, can a frail pen describe her heavenly beauty - this "glorious mirror of celestial grace"? She is a mighty huntress, pursuing the leopard. She is dressed in white, with golden adornments; she has yellow locks like golden wire. She is like Diana herself, or the Queen of the Amazons. She is Belphoebe!

She asks Trompart, whether he has seen a deer that she has wounded. She is about to cast her spear into the bush, for she sees something moving (Braggadocchio). In the nick of time Trompart identifies his boastful master. Braggadocchio shakes his "lofty crest" just as if he had been sleeping!

Braggadocchio is amazed that such a stunning creature does not reside at court but rather chooses to roam the forest. Belphoebe has no satisfaction in pursuing pleasure for its own sake. She says that before his happy mansion "high God did Sweat ordain." Braggadocchio attempts to embrace Belphoebe, but, lifting her javelin (spear), she scares him half to death. Braggadocchio tells Trompart that supernatural powers alone have been able to shake his courage, and conveniently he puts Belphoebe in that classification! So ends this comic interlude of Spenser's.

Canto IV

Sir Guyon sees a madman cruelly dragging and beating a handsome "stripling." Behind the madman hurries a lame hag with a staff. She keeps shouting at the madman to beat the young man more, offering him her stick and gathering stones. Sir Guyon tries to stop the madman who fights like a blindfolded bull. The madman knows nothing of the etiquette of courtly warfare, and Guyon becomes more and more puzzled about how to control him.

The palmer cries out that Guyon is fighting a monster called Furor that cannot be mastered or controlled, and that the old hag is his mother, Occasion. The hag has to be tamed before anything can be done with the son. Sir Guyon manages to get hold of the hag's tongue, fastening a firm lock on it, and ties her arms to a stake. Then he masters Furor and puts him in iron chains.

Then he attends to the young squire, named Phedon, the victim of Furor's beatings. Phedon tells a story of broken friendship and infidelity. His close friend, Philemon, had reported to him that Claribell, whom Phedon was to marry, had been unfaithful to him, with a groom of "low degree." Philemon managed to persuade Claribell's handmaid to impersonate her mistress, wearing her finery. Then Philemon himself assumed the groom's role, after arranging for Phedon to witness these events.

Phedon is led by these deceptions to slay his true, innocent love. But then the handmaid reveals the true state of facts. Phedon furious with Philemon's treachery, poisons him. Then he pursues the handmaid, with the determination to slay her.

At that point the madman, Furor, takes over the chase of Philemon himself. The palmer draws the moral of the story. The emotions have to be bridled before they become too strong for control.

They see Atin, the strife-stirrer, running towards them in a cloud of sweaty dust, "panting, breathless, hot." He wears a shield on his back, with a flaming fire in the midst of a bloody field and the motto "Burnt, I do burn." He carries two sharp and poisonous darts in his hand. He warns Sir Guyon to flee, else he will have to encounter the fearful Pyrochles, the brother of Cymochles, both sons of old Acrates and Despight (Self-indulgence and Malice). Atin is breathlessly running to catch up with Occasion. The palmer reproaches the "varlet" for seeking "Occasion to wrath." Atin goes off, having first thrown a poisoned dart at Sir Guyon, which misses its mark.

Canto V

Pyrochles, without saying a word, fiercely attacks Sir Guyon, who is on foot. Sir Guyon is nimble enough to turn aside from the blows, and strikes the head off the horse of Pyrochles, making Pyrochles fight on equal terms. Sir Guyon masters his opponent, but spares his life on promise of allegiance, and Pyrochles wonders at Guyon's "bounty" (goodness).

At the request of Pyrochles, Furor and Occasion are released into his custody. Occasion berates at once both Pyrochles and Guyon. Encouraged by his mother, Furor wants to fight his deliverer, Pyrochles! Occasion gives Furor a firebrand from the Stygian lake! Sir Guyon now has to rescue Pyrochles, whom he had just fought, in this mad, zany scene of nightmarish quality!

The palmer comments that Sir Guyon made a mistake through false pity in releasing these dangerous characters.

In the meantime troublemaker Atin has reported Pyrochles' defeat to his brother Cymochles. Cymochles had the unpleasant habit of hanging the carcasses of the many knights he had defeated on gallows trees, in honor of his "dame," vile enchantress Acrasia. At the moment he had put his arms aside and was enjoying himself amid a "flock of damsels." Atin spurs Cymochles on by asking what had become of great Achates' son whilst Pyrochles "lies on senseless ground?" Cymochles snaps out of his pleasures and immediately dons his armor.

Canto VI

Spenser observes

A harder lesson to learn continence In joyous pleasure than in grievous pain...

Cymochles, seeking to avenge his brother, comes to a river, on which floats a little Gondelay (gondola). In it a beautiful woman is singing and laughing to herself. Cymochles wants her to ferry him across the water. She willingly takes Cymochles but refuses Atin.

The gondelay sails without human guidance, avoiding rocks and shallows. The damsel entertains Cymochles with a wealth of stories. Cymochles soon forgets about war and revenge in her company. She reveals that she is Phaedria living on the "Idle" lake in a wide, inland sea. They reach a beautiful, fertile floating island, filled with flowers:

Trees, branches, birds, and songs were framed For to allure fraile mind to carelesse ease....

Phaedria sings of the beauties of nature, while Cymochles falls asleep in her lap. Nature does not work and strive, and why should man? Why should man waste "joyous" hours in needless pain, "seeking for danger and adventures vain?"

She leaves Cymochles asleep and goes back to the place where she first picked him up. She finds Sir Guyon, whom she takes aboard, and the Palmer, whom she refuses. Phaedria will have nothing to do either with the violent passions (Atin) or with wisdom (the Palmer). She entertains Sir Guyon as she did Cymochles. Guyon is courteous, but he knows how to draw the line when she goes too far. He is angry, however, when he discovers that she has brought him to her island and not to his destination! She shows him the delights and pleasures of the island, but Guyon is "wise, and wary of her will."

On waking up, Cymochles is not pleased to see Phaedria and Sir Guyon together. He challenges Guyon to battle, but Phaedria rushes in to intercede in the fierce fight that follows, arguing that it is better to spend the passing hours in "amours" than in these violent duels. On hearing her pleasant words, the contestants relent their rage.

She brings Guyon to his intended shore where he finds Atin before him. Atin at once insults him, claiming that Guyon had fled from Cymochles. In the meantime a knight, whose armor is soiled with blood, throws himself into the water, not caring anything about his safety. It is Pyrochles shouting "I burn, I burn, I burn" - not even the cold water can quench his flaming sides. Daily he dies, and daily he lives again! Atin tries to rescue him, but both get caught in the swampy waters. A man in an ancient gown with hoary locks comes upon the scene. It is our old friend, Archimago! He cures Pyrochles of the wounds Furor had inflicted upon him-wounds that caused his liver to swell and fire to burn his entrails.

Canto VII

Sir Guyon had lost contact with his trusty guide, the Palmer, since his adventure is Idle lake.

He meets a savage, his face tanned with smoke, with sooty head and beard, with coal-black hands. His iron coat is rusty, though underneath it is of gold covered with dust. He has a mass of coin in his lap which he keeps turning up and down. Round about him in the gloomy glade are great heaps of gold, ingots, plate.

This is Mammon, "God of the world and worldlings," but he trembles on seeing Sir Guyon. He richly rewards those who serve him; he can even supply crowns and kingdoms.

Sir Guyon regards such wealth as the source of all discontent. "Untroubled nature doth herself suffice." He argues that

The antique world, in his first flowring youth Found no defect in his Creator's grace...

but later ages abused nature's plenty.

Mammon and Sir Guyon engage in a long debate. Mammon leads him through a "darksome" way deep underground, and connected through a broad highway to hell, where sat Strife with a bloody knife and Pain with an iron whip. There also could be met Revenge, Despight, Treason, Hate, Jealousy, Fear, Sorrow. In fact, only a little step separated the House of Riches from the mouth of Hell!

Beyond Sir Guyon stalks a friend who hopes to seize his possible victim if he becomes covetous or careless enough to sleep. A huge cave has roof, floor, and walls of gold; but they do not shine, for light never enters the place. Chests of gold are strewn everywhere. Unfortunately, all the ground is scattered with skulls and dead men's bones! Through an iron door, Guyon sees in one place more gold than the world ever behold. In spite of all this, Guyon would prefer to spend his "fitting hours" in "arms and achievements brave."

Mammon takes him to another room where a hundred furnaces burn bright, tended by scores of devils, each one an expert in melting golden metal. They are amazed to see in such a place a warrior glittering in arms. But Sir Guyon rejects all this production and forcefully tells the "Money God"

……………what needeth mee To covet more than I have cause to use?

In another room he encounters a "villein" made of gold, carrying an iron club, named Disdain, striding big and tall, defying God himself, like a giant of the Titan's race. He wants to battle the knight, but Mammon restrains him. This new room is decorated with crowns and diadems. On a throne of sovereign majesty sits a woman clad in robes of royalty. Her beauty radiates brightness through the darkest shade. She holds a linked gold chain, the upper part reaching to heaven, the lower part to hell. People crowd to catch hold of the chain, symbol of ambition, each link being a step in the scramble for competitive success. Since all strive to keep the other fellow down, no one remains on top for very long.

The beautiful lady is Mammon's daughter, Philomene, and he offers her in marriage to the knight! But Guyon tactfully tells him that he has already pledged his love to another lady.

Mammon leads our hero to a garden full of leaves and blooms, all "direful black," fit to adorn the dead, such as Cypress, Poppy, Hellebore, Coloquintida, Hemlock. In this garden of Proserpine grows a tree so thickly strewn with golden apples that its trunk is concealed. These are the great apples that Herculesuhad sought; it is one of these apples that caused the discord, in the background of the Trojan war, between Venus, Juno, and Minerva. Guyon climbs the mound on which this tree is situated, and below sees the river of Cocytus full of damned souls, including Tantalus and Judas.

Guyon was on this exploratory tour of Mammon's kingdom for three days, and he was growing weak and pale from lack of food and sleep. Mammon had to bring him back to the upper world, for it was against the infernah rules to permit any living being to stay under the earth.

Canto VIII

Spenser praises the grace that God extends to his creatures through love. Bright squadrons of angels fight for mankind.

The palmer, who had been left behind by Phaedria when she took Sir Guyon to Idle island, approaches Sir Guyon, now in a trance after his visit to Mammon's underground kingdom.

Beside Sir Guyon sits a handsome young man like the God Phoebus with wings "decked with diverse plumes." This angel enjoins the palmer always to succor and defend the knight.

While aiding Sir Guyon, the palmer sees two paynim knights, Cymochles (fierce and fickle passion) and Pyrochles (wrath without cause), accompanied by an aged sire (Archimago again!) proceeded by the "light-foot" page, Atin. The sons of Acrates (self-indulgence) believe they see the corpse of Sir Guyon, and the palmer does not disabuse them. They want to despoil the corpse of its arms and shield. The palmer tries to dissuade them for the love of knighthood.

They do not complete their design before a knight appears with ebony lance and covered shield. He challenges them at once. Pyrochles, without his sword, wants the one that Archimago vanished to procure for Braggadocchio (Canto III). This is Arthur's own sword of metal mixed with meadow-wort, made by Merlin, against which there is no defense. Unfortunately for Pyrochles this sword could never be used against its rightful owner, Prince Arthur, and the stranger knight is Arthur himself!

Arthur kills Cymochles. Pyrochles continues the fight with renewed frenzy, but the palmer slips Guyon's sword into Arthur's hand. At first Arthur hesitates to strike Guyon's shield, used by Pyrochles, with the portrait of the Faerie Queen upon it. But Pyrochles, finding Arthur's own sword of no use to him, tries to crush Arthur with his two arms. Arthur is the stronger. Arthur offers to spare his life, if he will declare himself his liegeman. Pyrochles refuses, and Arthur, unlacing his helmet, strikes off his head. Guyon wakes to consciousness asking for his sword and shield, which are now available and are given to him.

Canto IX

Just as the Red Cross Knight visited the House of Holiness to complete his spiritual education, so Sir Guyon visits the House of Temperance.

Sir Guyon explains to Prince Arthur the meaning of the portrait on his shield. It is that of the Faerie Queene, the flower of grace and chastity, his liege, his sovereign and his "dear." Prince Arthur asks, how may a strange knight attain her service? Sir Guyon encourages Arthur, saying that he could easily be numbered among her Order of Maidenhead, as Arthegall (Justice) and Sophy (Wisdom) have been. No further mention is made of Sophy in the completed books of *The Faerie Queene*.

Arthur had seen Gloriana in a dream seven years ago, but since then he has had no sight of the "Goddess."

Sir Guyon tells Arthur of Acrasia, to avenge whose wicked deeds Guyon had been called away from the Court of Faery by the palmer.

They come to a castle, near a river in a pleasant dale. But it has been completely locked, long before nightfall. Arthur's squire shakes the building by blowing his horn under the castle walls. The guard, looking down from the highest spire, warns the knights to flee away, for thousands of enemies have been besieging the castle for the past seven years. And, just as he speaks, a thousand villains swarm about the knights, armed with unwieldy clubs, rusty knives, heated staves. But our champion knights rout them like scattered sheep.

After this victory, the knights are made welcome at the castle. The lady of the castle is unmarried, though she has had many suitors. She is dressed in white, her train of gold and pearl upheld by two damsels; her yellow golden hair crowned with a garland of roses.

She takes a tour of the castle with the knights. Its walls are so high that no foe can hope to climb it. It is built of the material that went into the Tower of Babel. It is partly circular in shape, partly rectangular-a combination, according to Spenser, of the imperfect, mortal, feminine, and of the immortal, perfect, masculine.

Alma ("the soul) entertains. Her steward, appropriately called Diet, has supervised the dinner. He has been aided by a chief called Concoction, and by an able assistant named Digestion. They manage everything with great skill, wasting nothing. The Marshall of the hall, Appetite, fortunately relieves this somewhat austere atmosphere by making guests cheerful!

Lovely ladies and "jolly" paramours behave themselves discreetly in innocent pastimes. Prince Arthur speaks to one lady, more melancholy than the others. He asks the meaning of the poplar branch that she is carrying. It is symbolic of herself-her name, Prays-desire. Sir Guyon meets a charming young lady named Shamefastness.

In the castle live three advisers who help the soul (Alma) to govern well. One, Phantastes, can foresee the future; a man of mature age, unnamed, is an expert on the present; the third, Eumnestes, knew the past. In the library of Eumnestes, older than Methuselah, the visitors discover antique genealogies entitled British Moniments and the Antiquities of Faery Lond.

Canto X

This canto outlines the genealogy of British Kings and of Elfin Emperors down to the time of Gloriana (Queen Elizabeth). The genealogy is partly mythical and legendary, partly historical. It is presented, from a historical point of view, uncritically. It was of interest to the people at the time, and is still of interest to scholars, but it, of course, lacks narrative excitement.

England was thought at one time to have been separated from the Celtic mainland, and had originally been called Albion. It was at one time inhabited by giants. They were deprived of its possession by Brutus, descending from the famed Aeneas. He had wandered to this western island, and his progeny ruled for seven hundred years. The manuscript that Sir Guyon read was "ample" and even Spenser did not have the leisure to repeat much of it.

Canto XI

Spenser reiterates his basic idea that peace and security can only exist where reason reigns supreme as in the case of Alma.

Guyon and the palmer come to a river and ferryman takes them out of sight.

In the meantime all the bobtail riffraff which Arthur and Guyon had dispersed before the castle of Alma had re-organized and returned to the attack. The captain, Maleger, has set up twelve companies.

Seven of them batter at the main castle gate (the seven deadly sins). The other five batter the five main bulwarks of the castle (the five senses-sight, hearing, smell, taste, sensual delight).

Prince Arthur and his squire go out from the castle to do battle. The captain, with deadly arrows such as Indians use, rushes about on a tiger that resembles a ghost whose grave-clothes were unbound. In place of a helmet, Maleger, pale with withered skin, wears a dead man's skull! Two swift-running hags, Impotence and Impatience, accompany the captain. Maleger moves so fast on his hideous beast that Arthur cannot get at him. At the same time Maleger lets go with his arrows.

Arthur has to play a waiting game, letting Maleger spend his store of arrows. Unfortunately one of the hags keeps picking up the arrows and returning them to Maleger. Eventually Arthur ties her up, but the other hag attacks him and nearly kills him. Arthur is just saved by his faithful squire, who snatches both "jades" before they can do further harm. Maleger, seeing Arthur lying on the ground, comes to finish him off, but Arthur recovers sufficiently to hit him with his mace. Maleger then lifts a huge stone, but Arthur drives his steel through him, half of it coming through his back. But not a drop of blood appeared! It is an understatement to say that Arthur was surprised.

So Arthur throws away his great sword Mordurre and his bright shield, and attacks Maleger with his bare hands. Arthur calls to mind that Maleger was the offspring of Earth. Whenever Maleger touched the earth, his life was restored. Arthur picks Maleger up in the air and keeps him there, carrying him for three furlongs until he comes to a lake. He throws the horror into it and lets him die. Impatience drowns herself, and Impotence mortally wounds herself with one of Maleger's darts.

Canto XII

Guyon and the palmer sailed for two days in the ferryman's boat. They pass the Gulf of Greediness, symbol of lustful luxury, and the Rock of Vile Reproach, symbol of unthrifty waste. If the unhappy traveler escapes the Gulf, he is likely to be dashed on the rock.

They manage to get by, and then see many wandering islands, unattached to any foundation. Fair and fruitful, with grassy plains and tall trees, they attract the wanderer. Upon one of these islands in the wide sea they see a pretty damsel combing her hair. She is Phaedria up to her old tricks. They pass the quicksands of Unthriftyhead, the whirlpool of decay. They see a ship sink laden with rich merchandise.

They come across acres of sea monsters such as "Dame Nature herself might fear to see." The palmer smites the sea with his staff, and they are gone. The palmer warns the knight of foolish pity as he had done before (Canto V), and Guyon ignores a maiden singing of some misfortune. Mermaids are another obstacle suitably circumnavigated. Suddenly they find visibility reduced to zero, and all sorts of evil birds attack them. Finally they reach land, where they are greeted by the bellowing of many wild animals. The palmer quiets them with his staff.

They reach the neighborhood of the famed Bower of Bliss. It contains everything that art can imitate; it is a world of painstaking counterfeit. Nothing is natural. The Bower does not fear the wild beasts-only Wisdom's power and Temperance's might.

The Bower is entered by a gate of precious ivory in which is carved with exquisite art the story of Jason and Medea and the Argonaut expedition. In the entrance sits Genius (not the Genius that is the power of life and generation, III, VI) who is the foe of everything alive and genuine. This Genius's staff does not represent power and rule, but is a mere formality in the garden of pleasure, where there is no ultimate purpose. This "false" Genius offers Guyon a bowl of wine which he declines.

The Bower is beautiful. Guyon himself wonders at "the fair aspect of that sweet place." They see a woman named Excess reaching for ruby and emerald grapes to squeeze into her gold cup. When the cup is offered to Sir Guyon, he throws it violently to the ground. A beautiful fountain is covered with ivy of purest gold "imitation" ivy, though expensive! A lake lies at the foot of the fountain with a bottom of bright jasper, the border set with laurel trees. Damsels are "disporting" in the pool. Guyon is briefly impressed, but the palmer rebukes those wandering eyes of his! As they approach the Bower of Bliss, they hear seductive music.:

For all that pleasing is to living eare Was there consorted in one harmonee: Birds, voices, instruments, winds, waters, all agree.

The silver sounding instruments did meet With the base murmure of the water's fall; And waters fall with difference discreet, Now soft, now loud, unto the wind did call; The gentle, warbling wind low answered to all.

In this world of painted flowers, trembling groves, crystal streams, they find Acrasia with her latest lover, a young man who has laid aside his honor and his warlike arms. In the background someone sings a "lovely lay" bemoaning, in a pagan way, the passing of time and beauty:

So passeth, in the passing of a day, Of martall life, the leafe, the bud, the flowre; No more doth flourish after first decay, That earst was sought to deck both bed and bowre Of many a lady, and many a Paramowre. Gather therfore the Rose whilest yet is prime, For soone comes age that will her pride deflowre; Gather the Rose of love whilest yet is time...

The Knight and the palmer rush upon the lovers and catch them in a net. They bind Acrasia with chains of adamant, but release the misled youth, Verdant. They methodically proceed to the total destruction of the Bower of Bliss. The wild beasts, which had formerly been men, until they had fallen under the spell of Acrasia, are restored to their former state. One man who has been a happy hog objects to recovering his manhood!

THE FAERIE QUEENE

TEXTUAL ANALYSIS

BOOK III

GENERAL THEME

The general **theme** of Book III is that of chastity. Spenser thinks of virtue in a positive, affirmative way, rather than in negative terms. Britomart's chastity is power rather than privation. While chastity might be considered in the Aristotelian system as a sub-division of Temperance, Spenser places this virtue in a special classification. It is certainly as much an "infused" gift from Heaven as a habit in the order of nature. Milton in his Comus reflects Spenser, in speaking of chastity:

She that hath that, is clad in complete steel, And like a quiver'd nymph with Arrows keen May trace huge forests and unharbord'd Heaths, Infamous hills and sandy perilous wilds...

Spenser presents many aspects of chastity and their respective opposites. Britomart's love for Artegall is highly romantic in origin, but gains full grown maturity through conflict and determination. In Belphoebe we have kindness and love allied to dedicated virginity. In the story of Amoret, her sister, we have the story of the woman perfectly reared for human love and marriage (Canto VI). Florimell presents a kind of heedless innocence, while Marinell symbolizes one yet unawakened to the meaning and power of love. His virginity is not one of choice, but of an immature indifference.

In Malecasta (Canto I), in the forester (Canto IV), in the churl (Canto VII), in the giantess Argante (Canto VII), in the Squire of Dames (Canto VII), in the old fisherman and Proteus (Canto VIII), above all in the story of Malbecco and Hellenore, we have various contradictions of chastity ranging from skepticism, worldly farce, to outright violence and monstrous perversion.

DETAILED SUMMARY AND ANALYSIS OF BOOK III

Canto I

Prince Arthur and Sir Guyon see on an open plain a knight and a squire, so old that "he" can scarcely carry his shield. The knight's shield has a lion "passant" (walking with one paw raised, looking to the right side) in a golden field. The squire is really Glauce, Britomart's old nurse. The knight knocks Sir Guyon off his horse through the use of a magic spear. Sir Guyon takes to the sword, but at this point the palmer intervenes, for he realizes the secret virtue and mortal power of that spear (Britomart's). The palmer persuades all parties to be reconciled.

Joining forces, they come to a very wild part of the forest, where only tracks of wild animals can be found. Out of this improbable place a lady, wearing garments of beaten gold, rushes in great fear and haste on a milk-white palfrey. She is pursued by a forester, intent on dishonoring her. Guyon and Arthur gallop off to rescue the lady, while Timias, Arthur's squire, follows in the rear to engage the uncouth forester in battle.

Britomart, not engaged in this adventure, comes to stately castle before the gate of which six knights are fighting one lone opponent. The latter does not yield a foot of ground. She separates the contestants, asking the cause of all their dissention. The six want the one man to yield all his claims to love a lady called the "Errant Damzell." Love, Britomart argues, cannot be compelled by "maistery" (force).

For soone as maistery comes sweet Love anone Taketh his nimble winges, and soone away is gone.

It seems that the lady of the castle, Malecasta ("Unchastity"), insists that any knight coming her way, who does not already have a lady, or a love, become her permanent "servant" in the courtly love sense, bound to observe her every wish. If he have a lady, he must forswear her, or else prove in combat that she is more beautiful than the lady of the castle. Britomart knocks four of the knights to the ground, and the other two surrender. As the winner of the battle, Britomart is entitled to the love of the "Lady of the Castle Joyous."

The group enters the castle with its rooms decorated with costly tapestries depicting love scenes from classical mythology. Lydian ("soft") harmonies are played, as squires and damsels revel and dance. They are entertained by the great lady, beautiful but "wanton." Malecasta falls in love with Britomart, believing she is a man, for Malecasta is a "weed" among roses, knowing no restraint. Britomart, without guile, treats her courteously and sympathetically. Malecasta homelessly goes to Britomart's room at night. Britomart awakes and not knowing who is beside her, reaches for her weapons. Malecasta shrieks, and the six knights, along with the Red Cross Knight, break in to see what is going on. One of the six knights wounds Britomart slightly with an arrow, but she and the Red Cross Knight put all to flight. Britomart and the Red Cross Knight leave the castle.

Canto II

Spenser, somewhat with tongue in cheek, states that in ancient times women won the chief garlands in war; that men, becoming envious, began to curb their liberty.

Traveling with her, the Red Cross Knight becomes interested in the reasons that brought Britomart to Faery Land. She is upset by his questioning, and this doughty female warrior begins to cry. She always preferred a life of hardship to that of pleasure:

Onely for honour and high regard Withouten respect of richesse or reward.

She then turns the questioning to the Red Cross Knight. She wants to have

Tydings of one that hath unto me donne Late fowle dishonour and reproachful spight, The which I seeke to wreake, and Arthegall he hight.

The Knight tells her that her impressions are wrong, that Artegall has the highest reputation. And the royal maid is secretly delighted to hear her love so praised; she rejoices like a mother who has given birth. She still pretends, however, that she wants to take revenge on him-only she can't find him. The knight says it is rather hopeless to match him in equal fight, and, as for finding him, he never stays in any one place, but roams the world aiding the distressed.

Actually Britomart had seen Artegall through a magic mirror that Merlin had created, which had been handed down in her family from King Ryence of South Wales. In her father's study one day, she looked in the magic mirror and saw her future husband, a knight all armed with his "ventayle" (helmet) up, so that she could outline the handsome face. He had a "couchant" ("lying down") hound upon a helmet fretted all with gold, with the motto: Achilles armes, which Arthegall did win. He had a sevenfold shield that had a white ermine and an azure field. Britomart falls in love at once with the image, going through all the painful processes of that experience, "sad, solemn, sour, full of fancies frail." She is sleepless and has frightening dreams.

Her old family retainer, her childhood nurse, Glauce, wonders

...................What evill plight Hath thee opprest, and with sad drearyhead Chaunged thy lively cheare, and living made thee dead?

She confesses to Glauce that she is in love with a man whose not want to feed on shadows while she dies for lack of food! Glauce advises her to fight against her passion, but, if she cannot, so that she only has a choice between life and death, Glauce will do everything to help find her knight. Before dawn, Britomart and her old family retainer go to church to pray for guidance. The nurse tries old-fashioned charms to cure her of her obsession, but they do not work.

Canto III

Spenser thinks of love as a sacred fire which has been kindled in the "eternal sphere" causing a man to choose virtue for "his dearest dame."

Whence spring all noble deedes and never dying fame.

It is this kind of love, also motivating women, which has caused Britomart to seek an "unknown paramour."

Glauce advises Britomart now to consult Merlin who had made the magic mirror in which she had seen the image of her love. Merlin would locate the man, even if he lived in Africa or the "Indian Peru."

Merlin, it seems, lives underneath the earth in a deep valley, away from all men's sight. By placing one's ear to the ground on the right spot, one can hear him and his one thousand spirits at work. Merlin, the greatest magician of all time, can make even the sun and moon obey him. He can even turn night into day, and create hosts of men out of the most insignificant objects.

Surprisingly enough, Merlin tells Glauce that Britomart needs a doctor more than his magic skill! Glauce stoutly maintains that her charge's illness exceeds the natural order. Merlin is amused, because he knew beforehand the cause of Britomart's trouble.

He prophesies that a famous progeny shall be born of Britomart's ancient Trojan blood which shall revive "the sleeping memory" of the antique peers. He identifies her marital partner as Artegall, a human being who had been stolen by the Faeries and taken into Faery Land. Actually unknown to himself, he is the son of a Cornish king. For a long time he shall be engaged in feats of arms before he becomes the father of her children. Merlin then outlines the historical fortunes of the various descendants of their "matrimonial bower." Eventually Queen Elizabeth herself will be born of this stock, the ruler of a united country after the long wars of Briton, Dane, and Norman. She will protect the "low" countries (modern Belgium, Netherlands), and decisively smite the power of Spain:

............Then shall a royall Virgin raine, which shall Stretch her white rod over the Belgicke shore, And the great Castle smite so sore withall That it shall make him shake, and shortly learn to fall.

After hearing this, Britomart and Glauce return home in a more cheerful frame of mind. Glauce then devises a foolhardy scheme. Since Britomart is tall and "large of limb," why should she not learn military skills and disguise herself as a knight? Britomart falls in with this scheme, coming to Faery Land, meeting the Red Cross Knight, and learning of Sir Artegall. Glauce may look like a very old squire, but she has plenty of pluck and enterprise.

Canto IV

Britomart formed a league of perpetual friendship with the Red Cross Knight after receiving the information about Artegall.

She eventually arrives at the sea coast. Her present squire and former nurse, Glauce, unlaces Britomart's helmet, and Britomart watches the surge beat against the rocky cliffs, reflecting her own feelings. Love has been her pilot, but he has been useless in heavy seas. She invokes the god of the winds to take her safely to her port, her destination.

Seeing someone hastily galloping towards her she re-arms. The stranger asks why she is trespassing along a forbidden route. He advises her to retreat before she is in trouble. "Let those flee who need to flee," replies the unimpressed Britomart. His words only scare children; she will pass or die.

The fight is on. She drives her wicked steel through the left side of her challenger, and he falls to the ground in his steaming gore. Britomart does not stay to help him. Along the shore she beholds pearls and precious stones; even the gravel is mixed with golden ore.

In the meantime, Cymoent, the mother of the critically wounded Marinell. hears of what has happened. She was the daughter of the sea god, Nereus, through a mortal mother. It was through her influence that the sea god had thrown up all these riches on the shore for Marinell. Cymoent had long feared that Marinell would lose his life through his martial aggressiveness. Proteus, a sea god famous for his capacity to change himself into the form of practically any living thing or any force, had prophesied that a virgin would seriously injure or kill her son, and the prophecy now seemed to have been fulfilled. Cymoent had warned Marinell, for this reason, against the love of women - "a lesson too hard for living clay." Many fair ladies had been attracted to Marinell, but he had never responded.

She and other water nymphs, throwing their garlands away, climb their sea-wagon, ride the billows, surprising all the grizzly monsters of the deep. Arriving near shore, schools of fish drive them along, to prevent injury to their feet! When Cymoent sees the condition of Marinell, she nearly dies with grief. Born of immortal seed, the mother sees the potential tragedy of the mortal son. What good is it to be immortal and see one's children die?

The nymphs are practical. They divest Marinell of his armor, clean his wound, pour in balm and nectar. One nymph, Liagore, has learned medicine from Apollo, the god of healing. She finds life still remaining in Marinell. Lifting him into their sea chariot, they go to the bottom of the sea to a giant underground vault, with a ceiling like the sky. Marinell is placed upon a couch, and Tryphon, the physician of the sea gods, is hastily called. The mother curses the hand of Britomart.

In the meantime Arthur and Sir Guyon are trying to catch up with the fearful damsel fleeing form the cruel forester. Coming to a fork in the path, they separate, taking different routes. Timias continues in pursuit of the forester.

Finally Prince Arthur catches sight of the errant damsel, but she fears Arthur no less than the forester. Night comes, and Arthur loses sight of her. Arthur goes to sleep. Sleep, says the poet, is the sister of death, is married to Herebus, the foe of all the gods. Night sends fear instead of rest, dreadful dreams rather than peace. Day reveals things in their true and honest colors; then the children of darkness are seen for what they are. Arthur awakes, troubled.

Canto V

Love affects people according to their character, Spenser says. It makes the base, baser; the noble, nobler.

Price Arthur comes upon a terrified dwarf. He has lost his lady, riding on a snow-white palfrey. Not a fairer person ever beheld the sun than this lady, Florimell. She loves Marinell, though he does not love her. Since Marinell has been missing for five days, Florimell has left the court, vowing never to return again until she finds him alive or dead. Arthur swears not to forsake the dwarf, until they hear some news of her.

Arthur misses Timias his squire, whom he loves so dearly. Timias did not have much luck in tracking the forester, whose intimate knowledge of the woods greatly helped him. The forester reaches his two brothers, the three of them "ingratious children of one graceless sire." Preparing vengeance for the squire, they wait in ambush for him as he crosses a ford. One throws a dart that pierces the squire's coat of mail.

Another forester keeps the squire from getting to shore by thrusting out a long boar spear. More arrows are shot at him as he struggles in the stream. Timias just can't get at his enemies. Finally he does. He terminates one with his spear; he cleaves the head of another in two; he beheads the third running away. Timias might be said to have had a good day, but the "the gentlest squire alive" has also been seriously wounded.

In the same wood dwelt Belphoebe who had put Braggadocchio in his place (Book II, iii). Hunting, she comes upon the unfortunate squire. She undoes his coat of mail and removes his helmet. An expert in herbs, she treats his wounds with, among other things, "divine tobacco" (a new discovery of Spenser's period)! On recovering consciousness, Timias believes that an angel is ministering to him, and he kisses her feet. The wood nymphs bring him to a valley, shaped like a stately theater surrounded by mountains and mighty woods, an earthly paradise. Belphoebe cures his physical wound, but inadvertently causes another kind of wound, for Timias falls in love with her. Timias talks aloud to himself about it. How can a simple squire reach up to his celestial creature? Belphoebe, chaste and courteous, a woman of "heroic mind," tends a rose that God had originally planted in Paradise, the symbol of Belphoebe's honor. She does not, however, give Timias the cordial of "that flower" which could restore a lovesick heart.

Canto VI

How could a creature like Belphoebe have been brought up in the rough woods far from court, the schoolmistress of all courtesy? The answer lies in her remarkable birth-Jove, Phoebus, the three Graces, all lavishing gifts upon her:

Her berth was of the wombe of morning dew And her conception of the joyous prime.

Her mother was Chrysogone who had also given birth to her twin sister, Amoretta. Belphoebe symbolizes unmarried virginal chastity; Amoret (for short), the chastity of married love. These sisters were begot by their mother without the intervention of man.

Puzzled and fearing disgrace at that time, Chrysogone had fled into the woods. It happened that Venus was looking for her missing son, Cupid. He was apt to leave home over small misunderstandings. She left her own home, from which are derived all the world's features of beauty, and sought Cupid in courts, cities, countryside. She suspected his hiding among the nymphs of Diana, the huntress. Diana was resting informally after the chase when Venus surprised her. The two goddesses were a little catty at first. Diana could not understand how Venus could find her way into such a wilderness! As for her son-she must miss him a lot, for he is such a help in her "disports." Venus replies

As you in woods and wanton wildernesse Your glory set to chance the salvage beasts, So my delight is all in joyfulnesse, In beds, in bowres, in banckets, and in feasts...

Diana, however, relents and joins Venus in looking for her son. They come upon Chrysogone just after she has given birth in her sleep to Belphoebe and Amoret. The goddesses each adopt one twin. Belphoebe is to be brought up in perfect virginity. Amoret, compensating Venus for her missing Cupid, was to be brought up in perfect womanhood, understanding human love.

Venus brings Amoret to the Garden of Adonis, where are contained the seeds of all things that are born and die. The entrance to the garden is guarded by Genius (the opposite of the false Genius in the Bower of Acrasia) who symbolizes natural generation. There are two gates, one letting people in; the other, out. Those who have died come back again, and those who are to be born go out. The garden is like a balance wheel-what goes out is balanced by what comes in. The stock of "being" is never lessened or increased. "Chaos" supplies the "substance" of nature's progenies. "Form" gives "substance" a body. The substance remains eternal, though the form comes and goes.

The great enemy to all the forms of being in the Garden of Adonis is "wicked Time." He mows everything down with his scythe indiscriminately. If it were not for time, everything in the garden would be happy. There is no rancor, no jealousy, and every paramour knows his lover.

In this beautiful place where the trees make an arbor through their own inclination (not forced as the Bower of Acrasia), Venus enjoys the company of her beloved Adonis. Adonis is "eternal in mutability," constant in a world of flux, for he is the father of all the forms that give life to all things. In mortal life he had apparently met death by the tusks of a wild boar, but Venus rescued him, and he lives eternally in a rocky cave underneath a mountain. Among his companion gods is Cupid. Psyche lives there too, the wife of Cupid, and they have a daughter-Pleasure. Venus brings Amoret to be brought up with Pleasure in the household of Cupid and Psyche. Amoret has become the guiding star of all chaste affection; and she now loves a noble knight, Sir Scudamour.

Canto VII

Meanwhile Florimell, though now free from danger with the death of the forester, has had such a fright that she still fears every shade, every noise. Her white palfrey is exhausted, and she has to proceed on foot. She sees a little smoke rising from the tops of some high trees, and comes upon a little cottage in a gloomy den. Florimell enters in, and the witch living in it makes clear that she is "unwelcomed" and "unsought." But Florimell is so beautiful that even the hag is briefly moved with compassion, and asks her to sit down and rest.

The witch has a lazy good-for-nothing son. Coming home in the evening, he looks at this beautiful creature like one who has unexpectedly come upon the sun!

Florimell adjusts herself to her surroundings, and is not snobbish. But the churl begins to develop a "base" affection for her. He brings her apples from the woods, tame birds, squirrels, garlands of flowers. Florimell, anticipating danger, plans to leave secretly. One day before dawn she departs. The churl, on discovering this, goes half-mad, tears his hair, bites his flesh, scratches his face. His mother does everything to "assuage the fury which his entrails tears." She turns to black magic.

The witch calls a beast out of her cave, monstrous, misshapen, hideous, somewhat resembling a hyena, and living on woman's flesh. The beast is instructed to bring Florimell back or to kill her. So Florimell is on the run again, pursued by a new nightmare. She reaches the sea, intending to drown herself if necessary. She finds a little boat with a fisherman in it asleep. She jumps in and pushes away from the land. The beast, afraid of water, has to satisfy itself with butchering and devouring Florimell's poor horse. Along comes Sir Satyrane, and, recognizing the carcass of the horse, fears that Florimell has met with disaster. He finds a golden girdle which Florimell has dropped in her flight. This is to become important in a subsequent story. He attacks the monster, inflicting many wounds, but is unable to kill it. Then he binds the animal with Florimell's girdle, and the beast becomes submissive.

Leading what seems to be a strange pet, he sees a giantess on a gray horse, with a dwarf, bound with wires, on her lap. She is fleeing from a knight. Satyrane has to set the beast at liberty, in order to fight the giantess.

The battle goes badly for Sir Satyrane. The giantess wields a great iron mace. His spear breaks in a thousand pieces on her shield. His efforts were about as effective as attacks on a marble pillar. She knocks him half unconscious, reaches her powerful hand for his collar, plucks him off his horse, put him athwart her own, like a piece of meat.

Meanwhile the knight who is pursuing her gets closer. Having to do battle with him, she throws her burdens aside. She turns apparently to fight her pursuer, then makes off again.

Sir Satyrane sights his new companion, a young man who seems a dwarf at a distance, especially in comparison to the giantess.

..................made fit for to deceive Fraille Ladies hearts with loves consuming rage...

Satyrane releases him from his fetters, and the young squire relates that the giantess named Argante was a daughter of the ancient Titan, Typhoeus, who, drunk through the blood of men he had slain, had committed incest with his mother, Earth. She has a twin incestuous brother, Olyphant. There is no limit to the sensual lusts of these two. The young man with the unusual title "Squire of Dames" refused to submit to the giantess because he had been vowed to the fair Columbell. The knight, now in pursuit of the giantess, named Sir Palladine, is a young virgin.

The Squire of Dames has an amusing, rather cynical story to tell. He had promised a special kind of service to his lady. In a year's time he was to bring back to his lady a list of all the adventures in which he had been involved with "gentle dames." At the end of that time, he brought back three hundred "pledges" of services for ladies, and their thanks. Whereupon his lady imposed some more conditions. He was now to bring back a list, equal in number, of ladies who refused his services and who remained ever "chaste and sound." Sir Satyrane was curious about the results.

The Squire had been refused by a courtesan, because he lacked money; by a nun, because he lacked discretion; and by a young woman of low social rank on the basis of ethical principle. The squire had become cynical about women; very few followed chastity for its own sake.

The beast meanwhile had wandered back to the witch, reporting on what happened to Folrimell.

Canto VIII

Spenser may well commiserate with poor Florimell's guiltless sorrows! The witch is exceedingly angry at the failure of her plan against Florimell She had hoped that Florimell was dead when she saw the golden girdle which Sir Satyrane had used as a leash on the monster.

She now constructs through her magic a false Florimell, exactly alike in external appearance to the true one. Spenser loves these juxtapositions of the false and the true. We have it in the case of the two Geniuses; in the two gardens, one of Adonis, one of the Bower of Bliss. The False Florimell is a robot managed by an evil spirit, skilled in counterfeiting the wiles of women. It is decked out in some of the clothes which the true Florimell had left behind. The witch's son mistakes the false for the true, and, of course, this time he is not resisted.

Braggadocchio comes along and demands that the churl yield the lady to him, and the churl is too cowardly to resist. Braggadocchio has scarcely finished making love to her when a fierce knight demands that the false Florimell be handed to him. Braggadocchio makes a gesture of defiance but then takes to flight. The new proprietor places the lady on Braggadocchio's horse.

In the meantime what has happened to the true Florimell? She has troubles-plenty of them. The old fisherman on the boat wakes up and think he is dreaming when he sees Florimell's blazing beauty. He behaves in an ungentlemanly was, places his hand upon her person, mingling passion with fish-scales! Shrieking, Florimell arouses Preteus, a sea god overseeing "Neptune's mighty herds." He rescues her, tying the old man to the wheels of his chariot and dragging him along. He brings Florimell to his bower at the bottom of the sea.

There he incessantly wooes her with speeches and gifts. Proteus was famed for his ability to change himself of many forms. Ulysses in Homer's **epic** had had to fight with him, and keep fast hold no matter what he changed himself into. Florimell says she is in love with a Faery knight. So Proteus becomes a Faery knight, but she will have none of him. He then tries more fearful psychological measures. He is a giant, a devil, a centaur. He gives up, and throws Florimell into a deep dungeon.

In the meantime Satyrane and the Squire of Dames set out to find the witch's hyena. They meet Sir Paridell who, along with other knights, has been sent out from Faery Court to rescue Florimell. Satyrane informs him of the discovery of the dead horse and of Florimell's golden girdle.

They come together to a castle where they are refused entrance.

Canto IX

Spenser hopes that he will not offend "redoubted Knights and honorable Dames," the specific audience for which he writes, by telling a story about a "wanton" lady., After all, one can also learn about good by an example of the bad.

The reason why Paridell, Satyrane, the Squire of Dames are not hospitably received is that the castle is owned by "a crabbed churl" who likes to live to himself. He is a miser accumulating "pelf," married to a beautiful woman younger than himself. She wants to "play among her peers" and to be free of the old man's jealousy. The old man, Malbecco, does not trust his wife, Hellenore, and wants to keep her away from company. Sir Satyrane considers the situation of this couple a hopeless one, for a woman's cunning can even deceive Argus who, in the classical mythology, had a hundred eyes. Unless a man possess a woman's faith and good will, there is nothing he can do.

Malbecco pretends to be the porter of his own castle, and claims that the master of the house, who has the keys, is in bed. Paridell, angered that the laws of medieval hospitality are broken, threatens him. Another knight, not of Satyrane's party, arrives and is also refused by Malbecco.

The stranger then tries to enter the shed where Satyrane and Paridell have put up for the night. They say they have no room, whereupon the stranger challenges them. Paridell responds, and, after some blows have been exchanged, during which Paridell is unseated from his horse, Satyrane pacifies the contestants. They all want to wreak vengeance on Malbecco. Malbecco, now seeing that they may burn down the castle gate, assures them that he is sorry for what the servant has done (really Malbecco himself!). Though the knights don't really believe it, they pretend to accept Malbecco's excuse.

They undress out of their armor, and the stranger knight lets down golden hair reaches to the heels! She is really Britomart!

Malbecco invites the company to have dinner with him and his wife. Satyrane sits before Hellenore, Sir Paridell beside her. Paridell plays a coy, seductive game. He and Hellenore have mutually transferred understandable messages though "a sacrament profane in mystery of wine."

The conversation at dinner turns to the subject of genealogy. Paridell explains that his ancestry goes back to the Trojan War, for he is a descendant of that Paris who had abducted Helen of Troy. We soon discover him reviving in his conduct some of the family traditions! Britomart tells the story of how Aeneas went to Lybia and Latium. Rome became Troy reborn. But there was to be a third Troy to equal both the old Troy and the Roman Troy. This is the Troynovant (London) of the exploring Trojan, Brutus. Brutus had accidentally killed his father Silvius, and, as a result, had gone with other young men over the ocean. While this antiquarian conversation is going on, the private understanding between Paridell and Hellenore gathers intensity.

Canto X

The tragi-comedy of the Malbecco story is under way. The next morning Paridell complains that he cannot ride out with the other knights because of the injury he had received at the hands of Britomart. Malbecco is not pleased, for he fears three things - the loss of his money, the loss of his wife, and death itself. He does not permit his wife out of sight. But Paridell can keep better watch than he! Paridell says nothing that, on the surface, could be construed to be a breach of hospitality. Yet there is a secret code in his words which Hellenore understands.

One evening Hellenore went to Malbecco's private room where all his countless wealth lay hid. She took what she wanted and set fire to the rest. She then ran into her lover's arms, crying for help "when the time for help was past."

Now Malbecco was in a terrible dilemma. Should he rush to put out the fire or rush to prevent his wife absconding with her new lover? At one moment love overcomes money; at another, money overcomes love. In this confusion, the lovers make their plans and flee into the darkness.

Malbecco disguises himself as a poor pilgrim, and seeks for Hellenore by sea and land. But she is too smart to let Malbecco find her trail.

Malbecco runs into Braggadocchio and the usual funny routine follows. He and Trompart trick Malbecco into parting with his wealth. They run into Paridell riding by himself, having already deserted Hellenore. His habit is to seduce women, and then lose interest in them.

A crowd of satyrs come along dancing and singing to noisy bagpipes. In their midst is Hellenore crowned with garlands! Malbecco watches the proceedings concealed behind a hedge, and watches all the satyrs kiss his wife in turn. At night, when the satyrs are asleep, he makes a half-hearted attempt to rescue his wife. But his wife prefers the loosely behaved satyrs to her husband's company. Driven by grief, jealousy, hurt pride, he runs without purpose like the wind. He comes to a cliff overlooking the sea. He throws himself over, but he has becomes so light and thin from frustration and worry that he is not injured. He finds a cave and creeps into it. There, by the boisterous sea, he never sleeps, always keeping an eye open. Feeding on toads and frogs, he has trouble with his gall and liver. He has ceased to be a man and has become Jealousy itself!

Canto XI

Britomart and Sir Satyrane, after leaving Malbecco's inhospitable house, where Paridell remained behind, meet a young man who has fled from the giant Olyphant, who is quite as awful as his sister Argante, whom we previously met. He fears not Satyrane, but Britomart, the flower of chastity.

Britomart, pursuing the giantess, comes across Sir Scudamour lying on the grass-his armor and the shield bearing the image of Cupid all to one side. He is moaning, calling upon the Lord, asking why does justice sleep and no heed paid to the cause of good men. Why has Amoret been kept a prisoner by the enchanter Busirane for the past seven months? Britomart, full of compassion for his grief, counsels him, and promises to aid him.

They come to the gate of a castle, protected by flaming fire, stinking of sulphur. Britomart places her ample shield before her face, divides the flames by swinging her sword right and left. Sir Scudamour tries to do the same, but the flames intensify and drive him back. He throws himself on the ground in despair and frustration.

Britomart reaches the furthermost rooms of the castle, rich with golden tapestries telling of the illicit loves of the gods. At the upper end of a great room is a massy gold image of Cupid, who is the victor over gods as well as men. She finds written over one of the doors, Be Bold. Entering another room, more gorgeous than the first, "wrought with wild antiques" in rich metals, she comes across another door on which is written Be not too bold. She stays there until nightfall but never sees a living creature. She is constantly on guard, never thinking of removing her heavy armor.

Canto XII

At night she hears a shrill trumpet sounding aloud, then thunder, and an earthquake that seems to shake the earth's foundations. A whirlwind blows open the door with the inscription Be not too bold. A "grave personage" on a stage set is revealed, bearing a laurel branch, dressed in a costume suited to tragic performances. He makes a speech like the prologue to a play. Musicians, poets, a masque come in due order. A most "delicious" harmony is played. Comes Fancy (mental disposition to "amorousness") dressed in painted plumes waving a fan; then his older brother, Desire, blowing sparks and flames. He is accompanied by Danger with a net and rusty blade. Fear attends, armed from head to foot, but terrified of every shadow. Hope, in silk samite, her fair locks woven in gold, casts dew from a holy water sprinkler. Dissemblance, gentle and mild, walks with Suspect, ill-favored and grim, holding a lattice before his eyes through which he peeps. Grief, dressed in black, Fury, in torn rags, Displeasure with a wasp, Pleasance with a honey bee attend. A beautiful lady is led in by Despight and Cruelty. A knife is stuck deeply in her breast, and her white skin is covered with blood. Her heart is extracted from her and placed in a silver basin.

Next comes Cupid himself on a ravenous lion. He has removed the characteristic blindfold from his eyes to enjoy the torments of the lady; he shakes his dreadful darts. Behind him come Reproach, Repentance, Shame, and a rabble containing among others Care, Unthriftyhead, Lewd Loss of Time, Sorrow, Change, Disloyalty, Riotousness, Dread of Heavenly Vengeance, Poverty, Death with Infamy.

As soon as these remarkable guests were assembled, a stormy blast locks the door so that Britomart cannot enter. She decides to wait until the next day when the masque will be renewed. But when time comes for the door to blow open again, she finds the "woeful lady" alone, bound with iron chains to a pillar. Before he sits a vile enchanter, writing strange figures with blood dropping from her dying heart. Strangely, Busirane is trying to make her love him! When he sees Britomart, he rushes toward his victim to slay her. Britomart, striking two blows, is about to kill him, when the lady shouts to **refrain**, for the enchanter must remain alive to undo the enchantment. Busirane is forced to do this, and Amoret is restored to health. And the enchanter is now bound with the terrible chain himself. Returning back, Britomart finds that all the gorgeous rooms have disappeared, as did the flames from the entrance. When Britomart comes out of the castle, she finds that Scudamour and the squire have left, believing that she was dead.

What Britomart has seen is an evil enchanter's false version of Cupid. This is not the true Cupid of the Garden of Adonis of Canto VI or of the Temple of Venus (IV, x). Britomart, chastity itself, has dispersed a perverted fantasy of what love between man and woman truly means. Scudamour himself carries the shield of the true Cupid. Spenser reiterates the opposition of true and false sentiments.

THE FAERIE QUEENE

TEXTUAL ANALYSIS

BOOK IV

GENERAL THEME

The general **theme** of Book IV is Friendship. A frequent subject of Renaissance debate is the question of the relative values of friendship, whether friendship should not rank higher than the love between man and woman. The latter is made possible by powerful instincts, but friendship is a work of sustained discipline, of disinterested generosity, unaided by the powerful urgings of natural forces. Do friends supplement one another's lacks and deficiencies; or is true friendship only possible among equals? Plato raises some of these questions in his Dialogues, and a more than usual interest in friendship as an art and vocation is part of the literature of the time.

Spenser illustrates friendship among equals in the central **theme** story of Cambell and Triamond and of their wives, Canacee and Cambine, and in the devotion of the triplet brothers to one another. In contrast to the feigned friendships of the Paridells and Blandamours, he illustrates the steady faithfulness of a Glauce to a Britomart, of a Timias to a Belphoebe, of a Placidas to an Amyas. He illustrates friendship between unequals (Glauce and Britomart), between man and woman (Timias and Belphoebe), between men, Placidas and Amyas. Spenser states in Canto IX that "love of soul doth love of body pass." and thus he ranks friendship above natural affection and sexual passion.

Aristotle listed three kinds of friendship. The lowest is based on reciprocal self-interest, and tends to disappear when the sources of advantage wither. The second kind is based on the superficial characteristics of a person-qualities that give mutual pleasure. The highest kind of friendship is disinterested, in which a person is loved for his own sake, not as the object of another's own good or advantage.

Higher still is the friendship based on the Christian concept of charity, in which the effort is made to love one's neighbor with the compassion of Christ. This is partly expressed in the legend of Courtesy.

DETAILED SUMMARY AND ANALYSIS OF BOOK IV

Canto I

Spenser says that grave men, absorbed with affairs of state, have criticized him for talking too much about love. Yet love is the root of all honor and virtue.

The enchanter Busirane had abducted Amoret on her wedding day when she was taking part in the enactment of a masque similar to the one previously described. Though Scudamour had won Amoret in single combat against twenty knights, he had never enjoyed a day of wedded life. Because Amoret would not submit to Busirane, he had kept her a prisoner for seven months, until Britomart had rescued her. Under the impression that Britomart is a man, Amoret still feels insecure as the virgin wife of another.

They come to a castle where a tournament is to be held. A "jolly" knight claims Amoret for his love, but Britomart overthrows him. Britomart unlooses her helmet, revealing a wealth of golden hair like a shining sky on a summer night. All are amazed, but now Amoret loses her sense of fear. She continues to travel with Britomart.

They meet two armed knights. One is accompanied by the wicked Duessa; the other, by Ate, mother of debate and dissention. Her home is near Hell; many roads lead to her dwelling, but none leads out of it. Her house is filled with relics of all the **catastrophes** of the past, of brothers forsworn, friendship broken, lovers parted. She sows the seeds of evil deeds and "factious words," and lives on their growth.

Ate has squinting eyes going in opposite directions, a tongue divided into two parts, each contending with the other. She not only speaks double; she hears double! Not only does she have deformed, unmatching ears, but she has feet, the one going forward while the other goes backward, and her hands work in contrary directions. She maligns God because He has been so good to His creatures. Her ambition is to destroy Concord and that great golden Chain of Being holding the universe together.

Duessa has a new knight, whose very name "Blandamour" indicates a smooth infidelity. Paridell, equally unstable, travels with them. Blandamour suggests that Paridell can get a lovely maid for himself in the person of Britomart. Paridell does not enjoy the joke, remembering how Britomart had unhorsed him before the entrance to Malbecco's castle. Sir Blandamour then tells him he can have Duessa; Blandamour himself intends to win Britomart. But Blandamour is soon disillusioned, for Britomart knocks him down, and does not bother with him any further.

Next, Blandamour and Paridell run into Sir Scudamour. Paridell, hoping to recover his prestige, attacks Scudamour, and both are unseated. Paridell has the worst of it; his aids have some trouble in restoring him to consciousness while Scudamour wants to continue the battle. Blandamour makes some nasty remarks about Scudamour's sportsmanship; this almost leads to more trouble, but Duessa intervenes. Ate exercises her genius for discord. She spreads scandal about Amoret, charging her with committing adultery with Britomart. Glauce (who has been accompanying Scudamour) quakes with fear. Sir Scudamour would have almost killed Glauce, so angry he was, and so ready to believe Ate's lies.

Canto II

Only a god or a godlike man, Spenser asserts, such as the great musician Orpheus, or the psalmist David who drove melancholy from the spirit of Saul, can defeat Discord, the "firebrand of hell." Glauce, who is able to exert a good influence on Scudamour, is in this select class.

Blandamour and Paridell had scorned Glauce while, ironically, they had taken as their own companions a fiend of a witch (Duessa) and a devil encounter Sir Ferragh who had seized the False Florimell from Braggadocchio (III, vii). Blandamour attacks Ferragh before he is ready, and abducts the new conquest, False Florimell. He gloats over his victory before

Paridell. Blandamour thinks he has a "peerless paragon" but, in reality, he has only collected another "phony." This is the fate of Blandamour, who, thinking he is so skilled in deceiving women, is himself deceived. Ate busies herself in infuriating Paridell against Blandamour, for the latter had failed in friendship by not sharing the False Florimell with him. A terrific battle is joined, the more malicious because of "feigned friendship which they vowed before." The False Florimell, instead of trying to stop the fight, bids them continue "for honor of their love."

A this point, the Squire of Dames passes by, and asks the cause of the quarrel. When he hears that the fight is over Florimell, he tells them that Florimell is far away. Those present then point to the False Florimell, and the Squire of Dames is, upon seeing her, duped into believing that she is Florimell indeed. He tells the story of how Satyrane found Florimell's girdle, and how Satyrane is going to hold a solemn feast, to which all the lords are to bring their ladies. The lady who is declared the fairest will be awarded the girdle. Why not win glory together, defending Florimell's claim, rather than fighting one another?

On their way they meet Cambell and Triamond, with their wives, Canacee and Cambine. Chaucer, "well of English undefiled," had originally told the story of these knights. Canacee, the sister of Cambell, had been "schooled in every science and work of nature." She had not responded to her various suitors, and disastrous conflicts had developed among them. Cambell offered to fight the three "stoutest" suitors, and to award his sister to the one who could beat him, if such there were. Cambell had a tremendous advantage, a ring which restored all mortal wounds. This fact, known to all, discouraged many challengers.

But there were triplet brothers whose names were Priamond, Dyamond and Triamond. They had, as it were, one soul divided into three parts. Their mother, Agape, was skilled in secret knowledge. She had traveled to the dark abyss, where Demogorgon is walled in darkness, to make a request of the three Fates: Clotho, who held the distaff; Lachesis, who spun the thread of life; Atropos, who cut it. Agape persuades the Fates, who cannot alter their decrees, to permit the souls of her sons, if any one of them should die, to pass into the person of the next.

Canto III

Agape had bid her sons to love one another dearly, and they were "ennobled" by their mutual "courtesy."

These three accepted the challenge of Cambell for the hand of Canacee. Canacee, on a stately stage, comes to watch the battle. Gold scutcheons, banners, trumpets and clarions give color and gaiety to the deadly affair.

The battles of the three challengers are described in detail. Cambell drives his spear into the side of Priamond; it breaks off leaving its head in the wound. Cambell presses his advantage, cutting his opponent's throat. Priamond's soul passes on Dyamond who takes up the bloody battle, and meets with a like fate. Headless, Diamond continues even beyond the conventional end:

The headless tronke, as heedless of that stower, Stood still a while, and his fast footing kept...

Triamond, now the possessor of the souls of his brothers as well as his own, joins the battle with triple force. Cambell seems several times on the point of complete defeat, but his magic ring practically brings him back from the dead. Cambell manages to drive his sword through the arm-pit of his opponent so that the wound is visible from both sides. But Triamond inflicts a terrible wound on Cambell's head:

So both at once fell dead upon the field, And each to other seem'd the victorie to yield.

The judges decide that the battle is over; the marshalls of the field break up the lists, but the two apparently dead men rise up and start all over again!

In the midst of this a gold chariot appears, decorated with antique Persian ornaments, drawn by two grim lions. Sitting in it is a lady "passing fair." This is Triamond's sister, Cambine, bearing a rod of peace around which two serpents are wound, both crowned with one olive. In her other hand, she has a cup of Nepenthe, "a drink of sovereign grace," the wine of the gods. Mortal men, who are permitted to drink it, find eternal happiness. The combatants momentarily interrupt their bloody fray when they see her. When they resume, the lady throws herself on the ground in tears. After this fails to stop the battle, she smites the combatants lightly with her powerful wand, so that their swords fall from their hands. She offers them the Nepenthe. Having drunk it, the knights discover that their rancor turns to friendship. Canacee comes forward and greets Cambine courteously. What started as a wholesale slaughter has changed into perfect love. Triamond marries Canacee; Cambell, Cambine. After this extended flashback, concerning Cambell and Triamond is finished, Canto III ends. Canto IV brings us back to the point where Blandamour and Paridell encounter Cambell and Triamond.

Canto IV

The aggressive Blandamour, having been recently unhorsed by Britomart, is not looking for an immediate fight, but he can't overlook the opportunity to insult the party of Cambell and Cambine, Triamond and Canacee. The two knights immediately prepare themselves for battle, but Cambine is diplomatic enough to quiet the situation, reminding all of the forthcoming tourney for the girdle of Florimell.

Braggadocchio joins them. He is infuriated to see the False Florimell in the company of Blandamour, because he, Braggadocchio, had taken her from the witch's son. Braggadocchio claims her and Blandamour suggests they tilt for her, the loser to have the hag, Ate, until he is able to find something better. At this point, Braggadocchio finds an excuse to withdraw from the fight, saying that he would not endanger his life for such a hag! Braggadocchio thus shows himself so base that he is incapable of sustaining either enmity or friendship! At any rate, another crisis is thus avoided, and Cambell points out that they should all reserve their energies for the tournament, where everyone may fight as much as he pleases!

The ceremony of the tournament begins with Sir Satyrane bringing out the girdle, decorated with pearl and precious stone, in an ark of gold! Sir Satyrane awaits the first challenger.

He fights the pagan knight, Bruncheval. Satyrane, not doing very well, is then aided by Ferramont, who is immediately attacked by Sir Blandamour. Blandamour is unhorsed, and Sir Paridell comes to his aid. It is now Braggadocchio's turn to enter this bloody game, but he doesn't have the courage. Whereupon

Triamond rushes in, and takes care of Ferramont. And so begins the crashing, swirling melee! Sir Triamond dominates the field for a while, until Sir Satyrane, recovering from a fall, enters again and severely wounds Triamond. Sir Satyrane is adjudged the victor for the first day.

Sir Satyrane leads his field at the beginning of the second day, while Cambell leads the Triamond forces, wearing Triamond's shield. Cambell defeats Satyrane but is then attacked by a hundred knights. Though Cambell fights like a lion, it is not surprising that he is taken prisoner. Triamond, wounds or no wounds, enters the fray in Cambell's armor, and rescues his friend. Triamond and Cambell are adjudged victors for the second day.

On the third day, Sir Satyrane begins by surpassing all, and there were plenty of fierce knights present:

Ne was there knight that ever thought of armes, But that his utmost prowesse there made knowen; That by their many wounds, and carelesse harmes, By shivered speares, and swords all under strowen, By scattered shields was easie to be showne.

But then a stranger knight comes in-his horse covered with oak leaves and his armor with moss, his shield bearing the motto, Salvagesse sans finesse (roughly, "primitiveness without discrimination"). He may well be symbolic of the strength of the primitive, natural man in the artificially contrived world of the tournament. He overthrows seven knights before he even gets started. They call him the "Salvage Knights" (salvage is our word "savage"). He is really Artegall, who is to be the hero of Book V. He overthrows Cambell, Triamond, and Blandamour. The field would have been his, if it had not happened that, toward sunset, another stranger appeared. This was Britomart, who begins by defeating Artegall, and then knocks down in rapid succession Cambell, Triamond, and Blandamour.

Canto V

The ladies now have a contest of their own for the girdle of Florimell. This girdle was the source of chaste love and faithful wifehood for the woman who could wear it. It would not fit anyone who was not virtuous.

The judges decree that Britomart is the victor on the third day, which means that she is the victor of the entire tournament. It was to such a knight that the fairest lady was to be awarded. The knights proceed to exhibit their various ladies, and the festivities have the air of a "Miss Faery Land" contest. The False Florimell seems more beautiful than the true one. She is awarded the prize, but, unfortunately, however the girdle of chastity was fastened, it wouldn't stay on her. Amoret has no trouble with it, but the judges award the girdle to the False Florimell anyway. And the False Florimell is awarded to the victor of the tournament, Britomart, who refuses her in favor of Amoret. The "Salvage Knight" had second claim, but he had disappeared from the scene. Finally, Sir Satyrane accepts her.

But now Ate spreads dissension among the knights by stirring up a quarrel over the vexed question of whose is the right to the False Florimell. Sir Satyrane offers to place the False Florimell in the midst of the contenders, and allow the "Snowy Maid" to choose for herself. Left to her own devices, she chooses Braggadocchio.

Britomart takes Amoret away from this contentious scene. Britomart is still seeking her love, little knowing that she had exchanged blows with him in the tournament - that it was Artegall who wore the banner, "Salvagesse sans Finesse." And Amoret was seeking her Sir Scudamour, little knowing the scandal that Ate had spread about her. (Canto I).

In the meantime, Sir Scudamour is seeking revenge against Britomart, who, Ate has led him to think, has seduced Amoret. On his journey, he comes to a blacksmith's cottage. The blacksmith's name is Care, and his foundry is a real sweatshop; his workers do not even have time to talk to their visitor. Sir Scudamour tries to sleep in vain; he gets no relief from his own troubles, because the bellows and the hammers never stop. He cannot sleep. And, if for a moment his eyelids close, someone hits him on the helmet with an iron fist; the smith nips him on the side with a pair of red-hot tongs. Sir Scudamour is more than glad to get out of that place and take to the road, accompanied by the "aged squire," Glauce.

Canto VI

There is no easy medicine for the anguish of "the gentle heart," observes Spenser. Scudamour encounters the "salvage knight," Sir Artegall, who complains of the knight with "the ebon spear" (i.e., Britomart) who defeated him and then took away the fairest lady, Amoret. Scudamour knows it is Britomart Artegall is seeking, although he fails to realize that she is a woman.

Suddenly they see their supposed mutual enemy riding toward them. Sir Scudamour attacks first, and is promptly unseated. Sir Artegall fares no better. But he fights on foot, and compels Britomart to dismount as well. In the course of a prolonged battle, Artegall manages to knock off part of her helmet:

With that her angels face, unseene afore, Like to the ruddie morne appeard in sight...

And her golden hair becomes loose, "framed in a goldsmith's forge with cunning hand." Stuck with wonder, Sir Artegall begs pardon on his knees. Sir Scudamour, coming near, is no less impressed. The knights lift their beavers, and Glauce hastens forward to explain things. Britomart recognizes the face of Artegall as the one she had recognized in the magic mirror! Glauce warns Artegall not to be "rebellious unto love," and asks Britomart to "grant him grace."

Scudamour, realizing that there was no truth in the scandal of Ate, asks news of Amoret. Britomart explains how she has protected her, only to have Amoret stray and become lost while Britomart was asleep.

Artegall wooes Britomart and she consents to engage her troth to him. Much to her unhappiness, he has to take leave of her and follow the adventures assigned to him by the Queen of Faery. Meanwhile Scudamour searches everywhere for Amoret.

Canto VII

Amoret had been seized by a wild monster that faintly resembled a man, but was overgrown with hair and had tusked teeth like those of a boar. He lived on the flesh of men and beasts. His lower lip was like a deep bag, holding the bloody remains of his various feasts. He takes her to his cave, where, as may be expected, she is half-dead with fright.

In the darkness she hears a stranger talking to her. This stranger wishes to die, but cannot. The stranger is a girl who also has been made a prisoner, along with an old woman, by this sub-human wildman who violates women and then eats them. This girl of high station had planned secretly to elope with a squire of low degree, whose father disapproved of the match. Before meeting her lover, Aemylia was seized by this "carle of hellish kind." The churl comes into the cave to proceed with his routine, but Amoret flees with all her might. The churl follows after. Fortunately Belphoebe comes to a part of the forest where with her wood nymphs she is hunting the leopard and the bear. Prince Arthur's Squire, Timias, who had remained in Belphoebe's company since his injuries in the slaughterous fight with the forester and his two brothers, (III, v) was also on the expedition when he heard Amoret's shrieks. He rushes to her aid, but the wild churl uses Amoret as a living shield in the fight, laughing aloud when she was wounded. Belphoebe hears the commotion and recues both Timias and Amoret. The "thing" won't stop to fight with her.

Belphoebe pursues and sends an arrow through its neck and throat as it reaches the door of its cave. Aemylia is freed. Belphoebe returns and discovers Timias kissing the unconscious Amoret, out of pity. Belphoebe refuses to have anything more to do with Timias. Timias adopts a melancholy, hermit-like existence. He throws away his arms, and takes no further interest in his appearance. Be begins to look wasted, like a ghost. Prince Arthur, passing by one day, does not recognize his own squire. But he sees a name engraven on all the surrounding trees-Belphoebe!

Canto VIII

One day a turtle-dove, who had lost her mate, came to keep company with Timias at his hut. A strong affinity developed between them. One day, when Timias was rummaging through various souvenirs he had of Belphoebe he found among them a ruby shaped like a heart, still bleeding from a wound. He tied it around the dove's neck. Whereupon the bird surprisingly flew away. The bird knowingly flew to Belphoebe.

Belphoebe recognizes the jewel as her own and tries to get it from the bird, but the bird keeps dodging her, constantly teasing her more and more in the direction of Timias. Belphoebe, meeting him, is full of pity for this unfortunate man, but still she does not recognize him. It is only when he makes clear that she is the cause of his plight that she understands and forgives. He resumes his life in "grace and good accord" with her, while Prince Arthur, his master, is still seeking him everywhere.

Prince Arthur comes upon Amoret and Aemylia and, through a precious liquor he owns, restores them to health. He places the ladies on his horse, and himself travels on foot. They come to a little cottage inhabited by a filthy and venomous old woman, gnawing her nails, and stuck with venom up to her throat. He name is Slander. She defames all good things.

Prince Arthur and the ladies have no alternative but to stay at Slander's place that night. The hag berates them for staying there without her consent. Spenser tells us that we should not consider the knight's presence with the ladies an impropriety because in "that antique age" people lived innocent lives in "truth and blameless chastity". Spenser does not bother to explain how the hag became a "contemporary" along with the other assorted horrors met in the course of the narrative. When Arthur's party leaves in the morning, the hag follows them, calling them "whores."

They see a squire galloping toward them bearing a shrieking dwarf. Chasing the squire is a giant on a camel. The giant sends fiery beams from his eyes that can kill at a distance. Remounting his horse, from which the ladies had been removed, Arthur manages to kill the giant, after the usual prolonged uncertainty. Even after the giant's head is struck from its body, its babbling tongue continues to blaspheme God!

The squire, Placidas, has a story to tell of this dead Corflambo. A squire of low rank had planned to marry Aemylia of high station secretly (the Aemylia whom Timias had saved and Arthur aided), because of the opposition of her friends. Corflambo, however, made the squire his prisoner before the marriage took place. Corflambo's daughter, Poeana, visiting her father's dungeon, fell in love with the Squire of Low Degree. In order to win some liberty, he responded. Though he won privileges, Poeana appointed the dwarf to keep watch on him, and hold the keys of the prison. The speaker, when he heard of the other squire's plight, goes to the prison to rescue him. He happened to be the exact double of the other squire in his appearance. The dwarf, making a mistaken identification, accuses this second squire of secretly stealing away from prison. Now mistaken for the Squire of Low Degree, Placidas is consigned to the dungeon where he contacts his faithful friend, Amyas. Placidas the next day substitutes himself for Amyas to visit the lady's bower, where he is well received by Poeana. One day, not knowing what to do with the dwarf, he simply snatches him up and flees away. Aemylia is delighted to hear that her lover is still alive, though Placidas, with all his tricks, had not managed to release him from the prison. But at least Corflambo is dead!

Canto IX

Spenser argues that "love of soul doth love of body pass." He ranks faithful friendship above natural affection and sexual passion. The story he is telling proves how Poeana rejected her father because of friendship with the squire, and Placidas rejected Poeana's favors because of Amyas.

Arthur makes Placidas walk in front of a horse as if he were a prisoner, and the unwilling dwarf is made to guide it. Corflambo's corpse is placed upright on it, with his severed head re-attached. The people at Corflambo's castle were deceived into thinking that there was nothing unusual, and the party was admitted without difficulty.

They find Poeana playing music, singing of her cruel love. Placidas is the one who fled, and apparently she did not know that Amyas, who had been cool towards her except as far as policy dictated, was still in her father's dungeon. The Squire of Low Degree, released by Arthur, is now seen side by side with his double, Placidas. Poeana does not know which of the two she truly loves. Arthur seizes the treasure of the castle, but permits Poeana her freedom. Arthur, in fact, goes out of his way to cheer her and bring her to a better frame of mind. He succeeds in persuading her to reform her ways and to marry Placidas. Henceforward, these two were to live in "peace and joyous bliss."

Arthur continues his journey with Amoret, who feels as safe in the company of Arthur "as in a sanctuary," because he has disciplined himself so well to the laws of reason. They come across Britomart and Scudamour standing to one side in a disorderly fight between Sir Druon, who cares nothing about the love of women, Claribell, who loves out of measure, Blandamour, who goes from woman to woman, and Paridell, who pursues anybody. They all symbolize perversions of the true nature of love. Stirred on by Ate and Duessa, they are quarreling about the False Florimell. The battle is extremely confusing because the various parties keep changing sides. It was amazing, the poet comments, to see such mortal malice among professed friends.

Suddenly, they all stop and turn their attack on Britomart and Scudamour. Britomart tries to argue them into sense, but without results. Prince Arthur himself intervenes, and forcibly breaks up this nonsense. After all, Arthur points out, Florimell (the false one, of course) should have the right to choose whom she wishes. A truce prevails, and Arthur, Britomart and Scudamour turn their attention to Amoret. Sir Scudamour is asked to give the background of her story.

Canto X

Sir Scudamour tells us that a pound of gall is always mixed with a dream of honey as far as love is concerned.

He had gone to the Temple of Venus (situated on a fortified island) to which there was only one bridge. Twenty knights protected it. In an open plain before the castle stood a pillar on which was placed the Shield of Love. Inscribed on it were the words:

Blessed the man that well can use his bliss: Whose ever be the shield, faire Amoret be his.

Sir Scudamour rapped on the shield, and defeated the twenty knights who came out to meet his challenge. He passed on to the outer gate of the castle where he encountered Doubt, with a double face, and Delay, who distracted visitors from their purpose. He got past these two safely and arrived at the Gate of Good Desert (Desert means "deserving"). There stood the Giant Danger whose main object was to frighten the wits out of visitors. Scudamour did not bother to bribe or cajole him, but assaulted him at once. Scudamour succeeded, and came to the beautiful island itself. Nature and art contributed their all to make it beautiful.

In its exquisite gardens, thousands of lovers walked. In another section, true friends conversed together. But Scudamour was not even distracted by these; he went straight up to the Temple of Venus. On the porch sat a lovable woman, but of very sober mood; she was flanked by two halfbrothers called Love and Hate. The woman's name was Concord, mother of Peace and true Friendship. Her task was to hold the planets in the courses the Almighty Maker first ordained. In the temple itself he saw a hundred altars buming sacrificial fire; the priestesses were young women. In the midst of this scene an idol, the Goddess herself, stood upon an altar that looked like crystal glass. She was covered with a veil. Her legs were bound together with a snake. The veil was worn, it was thought, because the idol combined both sexes in one.

One of the worshippers recited an eloquent prayer aloud, praising Venus as the queen of beauty and of grace, who fertilized the laughing heavens, the waters, the earth. She is the mother of laughter, the wellspring of bliss. At the foot of the idol stood Womanhood, Shamefastnesse, Cheerfulnesse, Modestie, Curtesie, Silence, Obedience. In the lap of Womanhood sat a girl in white:

Like to the Morne, when first her shyning face Hath to the gloomy world it selfe bewray'd: That same was fayrest Amoret in place...

Scudamour, inhibited and unfrightened, goes right up and takes hold of her hand. He leads her from the temple gate. Scudamour's shield bore the image of Cupid with his bow and shafts. His action here in the Temple was symbolic of his nature;

he avoided the pitfalls of love, and went straight to his objective with courage and honor.

Canto XI

Spenser returns briefly to the story of Florimell and Marinell. Proteus had imprisoned Florimell (because she would not submit to him) in a great rock walled with tempestuous waves and a thousand sea monsters. She spurned the god, because she was in love with Marinell; but he ruled women out of his life. Marinell was eventually cured of the wound that Britomart gave him on the wealth-laden shore (III, IV) by Tryphon, the "sea-surgeon of the gods." Canto XI is devoted to describing a great celebration held by the sea and river gods to honor the marriage of the Medway and the Thames. The roll-call of the water gods and the descriptive legends associated with the various waterways are long and detailed. Since the value of the writing here depends upon the exact language and **imagery** used, no purpose is served in abbreviating Spenser's content. Here the narrative line is for a time interrupted.

Canto XII

Spenser has realized what an "endless work in hand" it is "to count the sea's abundant progeny." Marinell, being the offspring of a mortal father and an immortal mother, could not partake in the banquet of the immortal gods. Wandering by himself, he hears under the hanging of a "hideous" cliff the melancholy voice of Florimell lamenting her situation. In her touching "complaint" she names Marinell as the cause of her sorrow. Marinell is torn with remorse and pity.

Marinell determines to rescue her, but he can find no way into or out of the prison. He develops a terrible sense of guilt, seeing himself as the cause of Florimell's troubles.

Coming home to his mother, he begins to lose his health, for he cannot sleep and he constantly mourns. His mother is worried, and wonders whether Tryphon had really cured her son of his wound. She brings Apollo, the King of healers. He diagnoses the case as not having physical causes; it is due to some inner anguish, probably love.

It was Proteus who had predicted Marinell's death through a maiden. That is why Marinell's mother had tried to keep him away from girls. Now that her son has told her that he loves Florimell, she goes directly to Neptune. He declares that it is none of Proteus's business to make such prophecies. She argues that it is Neptune's prerogative, and only Neptune's, to claim "waifs" upon the sea. He issues a warrant ordering the release of Florimell. When the mother sees her, she is delighted that Marinell is to have so beautiful a wife.

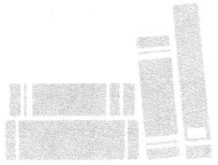

THE FAERIE QUEENE

TEXTUAL ANALYSIS

BOOK V

GENERAL THEME

Spenser in his succession of allegories is following a certain line of development. In dealing with Holiness in Book I, his **theme** is the preparation of the individual's soul for the communion with and understanding of God. In illustrating Temperance in Book II, he is showing how the individual must exercise sovereignty over himself. Books III and IV, dealing with love and friendship, assume that the moral lessons of the first two books have been learned. Now in Book V Spenser is concerned with man as a social being with a wide variety of relationships, in which he must always exercise Justice, in which he must always be certain that he gives every man what is due to him.

It is simple to say that a man should always do what is right, but it is not in all cases easy to say exactly what is right, nor is it clear how to judge a given situation. As one critic observes, "as the danger of the will is that it may be weak, so the danger of the judgment is that it may be deceived." Just as Guyon was betrayed by sentiment on occasion, so Artegall allows himself to be taken prisoner by Radigund (tyranny) in Canto V. Spenser shows Artegall acting in a juridical capacity in Canto where, meeting with contradictory witnesses, he traps the guilty part by causing him to reveal his inhumanity. In Canto IV he demonstrate the objectivity of a legal principle, showing that a man cannot invoke the law when it is to his advantage, and disregard it when it is not.

Artegall is accompanied by Talus, an "iron" man who is invincible. He represents enforcement of law, for, according to Spenser (Canto IV justice without the power to enforce it is useless.

DETAILED SUMMARY AND ANALYSIS OF BOOK V

Canto I

Spenser looks back to the dream of the golden age before corruption entered the life of mankind:

For during Saturnes ancient raigne it's sayd That all the world with goodnesse did abound: All loved vertue, no man was affrayd Of force, ne fraud in wight was to be found...

But in the world as we know it now, we have need of "the champion of true Justice, Artegall." The Faerie Queene has assigned this knight, who had been instructed by Astrea herself, the goddess who in the golden age had sealed the concord between gods and men, to rescue Irena (Ireland) from Grantorto (Spain). Astrea had given him a special sword, Chrysaor, which Jove himself had wielded against the ancient Titans. Along with this, she furnished an attendant, more formidable than any sword, Talus, "an iron man," "immovable, resistless, without end." Talus was equipped with an iron flail with which he could thresh out truth from falsehood.

Artegall and Talus, setting out on their assignment, see a squire standing beside a "headless lady," who wallows in her own blood. A knight had abducted the squire's lady, throwing his own lady from her horse. The dispossessed lady had followed after her own barbarous knight, and he had rewarded her in this final and drastic manner.

Artegall sent Talus after this knight, Sir Sanglier, identified by a broken sword in a background of blood on his shield. Captured, he is brought bound to Artegall. He denies everything. Artegall then displays his skill, not only in justice, but in the psychological manipulation of criminals. The squire and Sir Sanglier are each to possess and carry with him parts of the dead and of the living woman. Whoever objects to this decision shall carry the dead woman's head through the world for a year. Sanglier agrees to this decision; the squire rejects it. Whereupon Artegall awards the living lady to the squire, who, by his compassion, showed he was the true lover. Sir Sanglier is given the head-carrying doom.

Canto II

A dwarf informs Artegall of the forthcoming marriage of Marinell and Florimell. Sir Artegall would like to attend the ceremony, but, unfortunately, a Saracen, Pollente, guards a bridge on the way to the castle where the ceremony is to be performed. Pollente extracts tolls for crossing his bridge, which is full of booby traps. His daughter, Munera (Bribery), has been made a very wealthy woman by the "shakedowns" of her father. Artegall, after a terrific fight, kills Pollente. Talus is assigned the task of battering through the castle of Munera, who tries to delay Talus by pouring gold over the castle walls. Artegall approves his agent's action when, having captured Munera, he chops off her hands of bribery and her feet of unrighteousness, nailing them up as a warning. The rest of Munera's person is thrown over the castle wall to drown in the river below. Talus's execution of justice is indeed savage.

They see a giant on a rock holding a pair of scales in which he would weigh everything equally. He has a mammoth project "to share the wealth." Artegall argues that there is no point in such egalitarianism unless we can be assured that all things are on their "proper course" as they were in the golden age, immune from chance and change. Moreover, all things belong to God who can dispose of them as he wishes. And it is questionable whether all things can be weighed. Can you weigh the light of the East or the thoughts in a man's mind? The giant, on Artegall's urging, tries to weigh the false with the true. He finds that a gram of truth outweighs any amount of falsehood. The giant is not really seeking truth but merely trying to balance one extremity by another. He does not properly respect the "golden mean" where true justice lies.

Talus throws the giant off the rock to the sea where he drowns. It might be argued that the cases for and against the communist ideal are not properly presented here. The giant over-states his case by wanting to equalize, and therefore, measure everything, including values that cannot be measured. Sir Artegall overlooks the possibility that economic wealth might be measurable even if thought is not. In a certain sense, Artegall's "golden mean" is a measurement, too. Artegall ignores the reason why the "vulgar" - the masses - are attracted by the giant's philosophy. Angered by the slaying of their giant, the masses revolt. Artegall does not want to soil his noble hands with the "base blood of such a rascal crew." Talus is given the police task of slaughtering them. Artegall's sense of economic justice is more than right wing; it is obviously "Divine Right," even Bourbon!

Canto III

The marriage of Marinell and Florimell is celebrated with a great banquet and tournament. In the tournament, Artegall uses Braggadocchio's shield, and Braggadocchio wins the compliments for Artegall's actual feats. Braggadocchio boats that what "he" did that day was in honor of his own dame, the "false" Florimell. The Florimells, True and False, are confronted with one another. The "Snowy" substance of the False Florimell vanishes into nothing. Florimell's golden girdle is restored to her. Through another Solomon-like juridical maneuver of Sir Artegall, Sir Guyon retrieves his horse which Braggadocchio had stolen (II, III). The horse had an identification mark within its mouth, and only the true master could thrust his hand into the horse's mouth. The "counterfeit" Braggadocchio is "uncased" and then suitably punished by Talus.

Canto IV

Spenser argues that an understanding of justice without the power to enforce it is useless. For power is truly called "the right hand of Justice."

Artegall decides another knotty point of jurisprudence. Two brothers are arguing about a coffer of treasure that had been washed up on the sand by the sea. Their father, Milesio, had bequeathed two islands to Bracidas and Amitas. Most of the land of Bracidas had been eroded by the ocean, while the island of Amidas, through the action of the water had become larger. Amidas also steals Philtera, the betrothed of Bracidas. The former love of Amidas, Lucy, throws herself into the sea in despair, and chances on the strong box. Bracidas saves Lucy from the sea, and, in gratitude, she gives him the chest. In the meantime Philtera alleges that she had lost the coffer in a shipwreck. Artegall points out that Amidas had increased his land through the action of the sea. And it is the same act of the sea that brought good luck to Bracidas. Bracidas is declared the true possessor of the box, "for equal right in equal things doth stand."

Artegall comes across a group of warlike women about to hang a bound knight, Sir Turpine. Talus is sent into action and Sir Turpine is rescued. An Amazon, disappointed in love, wars against all knights. Her prisoners are made to wear women's clothing and do women's work. If a prisoner refuses, he is hanged. Sir Turpine had refused - thus, his present predicament. Artegall and Talus attack the castle of this Amazon, Radigund, who offers to engage in single combat with Artegall.

Canto V

In the course of a fierce battle, Artegall appears the winner, loosens the helmet of his opponent with the intention of beheading her. But pity prevents him from doing so when he sees her face, "a miracle of nature's goodly grace." While he hesitates, Radigund recovers, and attacks him. "So was he overcome, not overcome." Artegall, as the result of his mistaken compassion, yields his shield. He is taken prisoner, and poor Sir Turpine is hanged, after all.

But no one manages to lay hands on Talus! Talus, however, observes the feudal code. His master freely declared himself subject to Radigund, and Talus feels obliged to abide by his master's decision. Radigund develops a passion for her prisoner who refuses to respond. She employs her maid, Clarinda, to intercede for her, but Clarinda also falls in love with Artegall. Clarinda plays a double game, deceiving her mistress while trying to influence the knight. She tells Sir Artegall of her feelings, saying that if she found some favor in his sight, she might improve things for him (of course, she never really intends to free him). Artegall goes along with her, within the limits determined by his own loyalty to Britomart.

Canto VI

Talus brings news to Britomart of her lover's state. She is surprised that Artegall yielded instead of letting himself be overcome in battle, and, with mixed emotions of pity and anger, she sets out to rescue him. On her way she meets a peaceful and elderly knight who invites her to stay the night at his home. She does not disarm while stopping there, because she says she has taken a vow not to do so, until she has fulfilled revenge upon a mortal foe. Suspicious, Britomart stays awake all night, as does Talus. The bed, on which she was supposed to sleep, falls through a trap door! A group of armed men attack her bedroom door, but Talus more than takes care of them. Britomart waits for the morning light. The "host," Sir Dolan ("the deceiver"), had assumed that Britomart, because of the presence of Talus, was Artegall who had slain his deceitful son, Guizor. He comes down with his two remaining sons in the morning only to find that his guests have fled. Britomart subsequently slays the two sons on the same perilous bridge where Artegall had formerly killed Pollente.

Canto VII

Britomart comes to the Temple of Isis, where equity reigns. Equity implies a justice that modifies the letter of the law by an understanding of the total human situation. In the temple, Britomart has a mysterious vision of a crocodile lying at the foot of Isis, devouring a tempest and flames that strike the altar. The crocodile, proud of his power, threatens the goddess, but she calms him with a rod. He makes love to her instead, and out of their union a mighty lion is born. Britomart awakes frightened, but the priests interpret this strange dream of her. The crocodile is Osyris, "the justest man alive," sleeping at the foot of Isis. He is justice, but Isis is clemency. Artegall is like Osyris; Britomart is like Isis. He will destroy her foes as the crocodile destroyed tempests and flames. Britomart and Artegall will have a son like the lion.

Britomart fights a single combat with Radigund, slaying her, and Talus dispatches the other Amazons. Artegall is freed, but has to take leave of the saddened Britomart to resume the adventure assigned him by the Faerie Queene, the freeing of Irena.

Canto VIII

Love of woman can be a danger, Spenser reminds us, citing the story of King David, and that of Antony and Cleopatra.

Artegall sees a damsel fleeing from two knights. A third knight is chasing the other two. One knight stops to fight the pursuer, while the other continues in pursuit of the girl. The girl appeals to Sir Artegall for help. Artegall kills her immediate pursuer, and the third knight kills the second. Artegall breaks a spear with the third knight who fails to make the right identification. The girl fortunately clarifies the misunderstanding. In this odd and dangerous way, Artegall and Prince Arthur meet.

It seems that the damsel serves a famed princess named Mercila (Queen Elizabeth) who is under subversive attack from the Souldan (Spain), who has an evil wife named Adicia. The damsel, Samient, had been an ill-received messenger sent by Mercila to see whether some understanding might be possible with the Souldan. Adicia was responsible for sending the two knights in hot pursuit of Samient.

In planning suitable "avengement" against the Souldan and his lady, Sir Artegall disguises himself in the armor of one of the slain knights and makes it seem that he is leading Samient back as a prisoner. He is well received. Shortly thereafter, Prince Arthur arrives, sending a direct challenge to the Souldan. The fierce Souldan accepts at once, driving his chariot mounted with iron hooks and pulled by horses fed with the flesh of men half-dead! It is indeed a horrible battle, for Arthur can never get near enough to the Souldan to harm him. Finally, Arthur uncovers his magic shield; the horses panic, the Pagan cannot control them, and he is torn to pieces by the iron hooks on his own overthrown chariot. In the meantime, Artegall has protected Samient from the Souldan's wife, who has gone insane with frustration.

Canto IX

Samient wants to take the two victorious knights to see her mistress, Mercila. From information supplied by her they seek out a wicked villain named Malengin (Guile). Quick in tongue and hand, he is able to deceive men while looking them straight in the eye. He lives in a rock full of secret passages, one of which may lead straight down to Hell. The knights appear to offer the damsel as bait in front of the rock. Malengin comes out with an iron hook and a net to catch whatever he can, particularly fools. He catches Samient in the net, but finds his way back to the cave blocked by the two knights. Artegall and Talus cope with him, while Arthur watches the cave. Malengin changes into a fox, a bush, a bird, a stone, a hedgehog, a snake. The snake change is unsuccessful, and Talus flattens him out with his iron flail. They arrive in time at Mercila's castle to attend the trial of Duessa, charged by the Law of Nations, of Religion, and of Justice. Prince Arthur (seen here as the Earl of Leicester) had felt some compassion for Duessa (seen here as Mary, Queen of Scots) at one time, but is now convinced that she is guilty of murder, sedition, adultery. Mercila does not sentence her, though she has been found guilty.

Canto X

Spenser says in regard to justice that it is better to save than to destroy. Mercila was merciful, yet inviolate right ultimately demanded Duessa's execution.

Belgae (the Netherlands), the mother of seventeen children (the Dutch provinces) appeals for help against a tyrant Geryoneo (Spanish rule). Prince Arthur arrives in Belgae's land, and finds the towns desolate under the yoke of the Inquisition. Human sacrifice is offered to a cursed idol, under whose stone lies a dreadful monster. Prince Arthur proves his helpfulness to the oppressed people by capturing a castle.

Canto XI

Arthur slays Geryoneo and the monster.

Artegall, in the course of his journey, meets Sir Sergis who had originally accompanied Irena on her journey of petition to the Faery Court. Sir Sergis reports that if no champion appears in time to defend Irena (Ireland), Grantorto (Spain) will execute her. On the way they see a mob of people trying to make a knight their bondsman, while a lady in the distance weeps bitterly. Their numbers are so great that they force the knight, Sir Burbon (Henry of Navarre), to throw away his shield (Protestantism) and thus disgrace himself. (Henry, in order to succeed to the throne of France, had rejected Protestantism and had become a Catholic.) Sir Burbon argues

To temporize is not from truth to swerve Ne for advantage terme to entertaine...

Artegall cannot endure such thinking, but he still decides to aid Burbon against the aggressive rabble threatening him. Burbon recovers his lady, Flourdelis (France), whom he had betrayed by throwing away his shield. Artegall reproves her for accepting Burbon again so easily.

Canto XII

Artegall (also Arthur, Lord Grey of Wilton, under whom Spenser served in Ireland), accompanied by Talus and Sir Sergis, takes ship and finds hosts of men opposing his landing in the land of Irena (Ireland). To avoid needless slaughter Artegall challenges Grantorto (Spain) to single combat. Artegall beheads his enemy with his good sword, Chrysaor. Irena is freed, but before Artegall can reform her country thoroughly, he is recalled to Faery Court. On his return, the two old hags, Envy and Detraction, cause him a great deal of trouble. They have set the Blatant Beast to work, barking and baying through the universe.

THE FAERIE QUEENE

TEXTUAL ANALYSIS

BOOK VI

GENERAL THEME

Sir Artegall discovered in Book V that the administration of Justice is not so easy when it has to deal with vague and intangible elements such as Envy, Detraction, and the Blatant Beast. In fact, even Sir Calidore in Book VI tames the Blatant Beast for a limited period only.

The virtue opposite to the values expressed by slander and the verbal destructiveness of ill will is Courtesy. Courtesy reflects the positive power of Christian charity, the ability to imagine oneself in the place of another, to avoid needless hurt and injury-in brief, to love one's neighbor as oneself. While the word "courtesy" signifies the manners and **conventions** of a Court, Spenser is careful not to limit it to so narrow a context. As much as Spenser is attached to the idea of "gentle" (that is, noble, of high ranK) blood, he goes out of his way in Book VI to stress that the basis of Courtesy is truth and honesty, the avoidance of lies and flattery (Canto I). Of particular interest in this respect is his portrait of the "salvage man." This man not even know human language; he is completely ignorant of all the graces and utilities of civilized life. Yet it is very primitiveness which renders him immune to the Blatant Beast. If he is indeed uncivilized, he is therefore unaware of civilized vice and corruption. Representing the natural good in man, he always has the instinct for the right thing, and the natural energy to pursue it. For Spenser, wealth and luxury do not represent civilization-many of his evil characters abound in rich settings; true civilization is marked rather by sincerity and good acts. This is demonstrated in his pastoral in Cantos IX and X. Calidore goes beyond justice-he tries to give more than what is merely due to a person. He emulates Saint Charity!

DETAILED SUMMARY AND ANALYSIS OF BOOK VI

Canto I

Calidore was the most "courteous" of knights, loving simple truth and honesty, avoiding lies and flattery. His "hard" adventure is to subdue the Blatant Beast released (at the end of Book V) by Envy and Detraction to attack Sir Artegall.

He finds a squire bound hand and foot to a tree. The squire had to pass a castle where the "custom" was cut off a knight-errant's beard and shave his lady's head. Briana, the lady of the castle, cannot win the love of her ideal Knight, Crudor, until she presents him with a mantle made of the beard of knights and the locks of ladies. Upon hearing of this, Sir Calidore proceeds to slay Mallefort, the villain assigned to this discourteous task of barbering. Calidore tells Briana that there is no greater shame to man than discourtesy. Meeting Crudor in single combat,

Calidore defeats him, but spares his life on the latter's giving his firm word to reform his life. Crudor releases Briana from her commitment to present him with the mantle of hair, and they become happily betrothed.

Canto II

Sir Calidore sees a tall young man on foot, fighting a mounted knight. By the time Calidore reaches the combatants, the young man, about seventeen years of age, wearing a woodsman's green jacket, has killed his man. A fair lady, who was standing distraughtly near the combatants, was forced to go on foot, while the deceased knight had ridden, "thumping" his lady with a spear when she did not walk fast enough. The lady explains that her knight had come across an unarmed knight with a lady, had become desirous of the lady, made his own lady dismount, severely wounded the defenseless knight, whose lady fled into the wood. Foiled in his design, this wretched character expressed his frustration by treating his own lady in the way described. Sir Calidore, deeply impressed by the young man whose name is Tristram, son of former King Meliogras of Cornwall, dubs him a squire, and leaves the distraught lady in his charge. Coming across the severely wounded knight and the lady who has now returned to him, Calidore carries the knight on his shield to a neighboring castle.

Canto III

"The gentle mind by gentle deeds is known" says Spenser, and "gentle blood will gentle manners breed." Calidore brings the wounded knight, Aladine, back home to his elderly father, Aldus, a "retired" knight. Aladine's lady, Priscilla, has a further worry-not only is her knight badly wounded, but she fears some scandal may arise from the circumstances in which he met his misfortune. Sir Calidore takes her to her own home, and tactfully and persuasively assures her father that no impropriety had been committed. Going on his way, Calidore meets two lovers, a knight and his lady, Sir Calepine and Serena. While Calidore is engaged in pleasant conversation with Sir Calepine, Serena is seized by the Blatant Beast. Sir Calidore pursues the monster, forcing it to drop the lady. Sir Calepine finds his lady injured, puts her on his horse, and comes to a ford where he encounters another knight and lady.

Sir Calepine asks this knight to let him ride behind him on his horse for "safe conducting of his sickly lady." The knight refuses, thus angering his own lady who reproves him. He stands on the bank and laughs at Sir Calepine struggling in the water. Reaching the other side, Sir Calepine challenges this rude brute to fight on foot, but the challenge goes unheeded. Sir Calepine comes to a castle owned by this same knight, Sir Turpine (not to be confused with the Sir Turpine of V, iv, who was hanged), and is refused hospitality. Turpine's lady, Blandina, intercedes again, to no avail. Serena is forced to sleep outdoors in her wounded condition. Next morning Turpine attacks Calepine, pursues him (Calepine cannot fight because he must look after his injured wife, Serena), and strikes him through the shoulder.

Canto IV

Sir Calepine is suddenly rescued by a "salvage man." This curious character knows nothing of arms or the laws concerning them, but through magic he is invulnerable. He drives Turpine away terrified, and ministers to Serena and Calepine. He communicates with them by signs, for the salvage man does not know any language. Skilled in herbs, he tries to restore the battered couple to health. One day while Calepine is listening to the song of the thrushes, he sees a bear with an infant between his bloody jaws. He pursues the bear, forcing it to release its burden. Unarmed. Calepine thrusts a stone down the bear's throat, choking him to death! The child, miraculously, is uninjured. But now Sir Calepine finds himself lost in the forest. He runs into a lamenting woman, Matilde, wife of the childless Sir Bruin. Unless Sir Bruin has an heir, an enemy will inherit his lands. Yet it has been prophesied that he should have a son who would be gotten, not begotten! Sir Calepine persuades Matilde to take the child as her own, and thus the prophecy is fulfilled.

Canto V

The salvage man shows by his conduct, Spenser asserts, that he must have been born of noble blood. He still has not been able to cure Serena. Her wound, together with her husband's absence, brings her close to despair. She decides to leave, but the salvage man, wearing the arms of the absent Calepine, insists on going with her.

Prince Arthur and Timias encounter them. Timias, restored to high favor with Belphoebe (as Sir Walter Raleigh had been with Queen Elizabeth), had nevertheless developed strong enemies: Despetto (Malice), Decetto (Deceit), Defetto (Detraction). Timias had also been bitten by the Blatant Beast, while pursuing him. In continuing the chase, he had been ambushed by these three characters but was saved by Arthur. There had been a tremendous reconciliation, for Arthur had deeply missed Timias. But now Timias mistakenly attacks the salvage man who had laid aside his armor to repair some equipment on Serena's horse. Serena interposes, and the story of the salvage man's kindness is made known. The party comes to a hermitage, and the holy man, who had once been a famous knight, agrees to look after the two victims of the Blatant Beast, Serena and Timias.

Canto VI

The poisonous sting of the Blatant Beast was not curable by ordinary medicine. And the wound became worse by being neglected. The hermit trains Sarena and Timias in spiritual discipline, for the cure of their wounds has to come from the inner spirit.

Prince Arthur, aided by the salvage man, after a terrific battle with the forces of the Turpine household, forces Sir Turpine to yield, sparing his life only in answer to Blandina's pleas.

Canto VII

Prince Arthur had allowed pity to overcome him (as Sir Guyon and Sir Artegall had done on occasion), for Sir Turpine was a coward and a liar, whose surrender meant nothing. He tells a false story about Prince Arthur to two knights whom he persuades to do "justice" against Arthur. Arthur kills one, and is about to render the same service to the other, when the latter tells him of Turpine's guile. Arthur arranges for this knight to report to Turpine that Arthur is dead. This knight and Turpine arrive back to the place where to their surprise, Arthur lies asleep, unarmed. Turpine now tries to persuade his guide to kill Arthur, but this man remains true to his bargain. The salvage man returns; Arthur wakes up. They hang the pleading Turpine on a tree by the heels.

In the meantime, Serena and Timias, restored to health, journey together. They meet a beautiful maiden, clad in mourning, riding on a mangey jade, led by a "lewd" fool. This was a lady of rank, decked with "wondrous gifts of nature's grace." She had despised scores of lovers, and many complaints had been lodged against her at the Court of Cupid. This Mirabella was sentenced to roam through the world to save as many loves as she had rejected. After two years, she had not succeeded. Disdain, kinsman to the Orgoglio whom Prince Arthur slew in Book I, stalking on his toes like a crane, staring horribly, was her guide, while Scorn, the fool, whipped both her and the horse. Timias tries to rescue the lady, but Scorn takes him prisoner, ties his hands, leads him about on a rope and constantly beats him. Serena flees.

Canto VIII

Disdain, Scorn, Mirabella, and Timias run into Arthur and Sir Enias, the knight whom Turpine had tried to use against Arthur. Arthur, after a prolonged battle, is about to kill Disdain, when Mirabella surprisingly pleads for his life. She says that his death would mean that she would also have a "lamentable" end.

Arthur asks her why she carries a bottle in front and a bag on her back. Into the bottle she pours the tears of contribution, and into the bag, repentance for things past. Arthur releases the prisoner of Disdain, and finds that it is his own squire, Timias! Meanwhile the salvage man is about to tear Scorn to pieces, who had been getting the upper hand over Sir Enias, when Mirabella intercedes again for her other persecutor. Mirabella was beyond help; she had to go through with her penance, and Disdain and Scorn must accompany her.

Serena, who had fled when Timias became the prisoner of Disdain and Scorn, becomes a captive herself of a "salvage" nation-not kind savages but robbers and cannibals. Their appetites both for food and sex are destructive and unlimited. They have a religion of human sacrifice, and Serena is about to end her days as a votive offering in a barbarous religious rite, when she is saved just in time by the Sir Calepine, who suddenly appears.

Canto IX

Calidore continues to pursue the elusive Blatant Beast through countryside and town. Now comes a beautiful pastoral interlude, beloved by the Elizabethans. Spenser idealizes the simple life as it is led among honest and friendly shepherds and fair damsels; he depicts their garlands, village dancing, the playing of reed pipes, and the generous consumption of milk, cheese, and fruit. Calidore (also Sir Philip Sidney, author of the famous Arcadia) falls in love with Pastorella (Frances Walsingham, Sidney's wife) daughter of old Meliboe (Sir Francis Wallsingham).

The **theme** is, in Meliboe's words, that "wisdom is most riches." Calidore has a rival, Coridon, whom Calidore treats fairly and courteously.

Canto X

Calidore pretty well forgets the Blatant Beast in this pleasant land of innocence. In a beautiful section of the forest, Calidore has the rare privilege one day of seeing the three Graces dancing. In the midst of the ceremony is a shepherd lass (Spenser's own wife, Elizabeth Boyle) to whom Colin Clout (Spenser himself) pipes. But as soon as Calidore makes his presence known in this place of beauty, they vanish.

Calidore scores, without planning to do so, over his rival Coridon by bravely fighting a lion that had surprised Pastorella, while Coridon loses his courage. But there were worse dangers than lions in this idyllic land. Brigands invade Pastorella's country; they make all the villagers their prisoners, including Meliboe, Pastorella, and Coridon. They are imprisoned in caves of almost total darkness.

Canto XI

To Pastorella's lot now falls the share of troubles reserved for Spenser's heroines. The brigand chief wants Pastorella for himself. She does not respond, but, hoping to have some minimum liberty, she pretends some "show of favor." At this time merchants come to buy slaves from the brigands. The merchants will buy nothing unless Pastorella is included. But the brigands chief refuses to part with her. The other brigands are furious at the prospect of failing to make the sale. A terrific general melee ensues. Coridon escapes, but Meliboe is killed. Pastorella, though alive, is held in the arms of the dead chief, and both are covered with carcasses! The surviving brigands pull her out, and return her to imprisonment. Calidore hears from Coridon what has happened. He disguises himself as a poor shepherd, and is hired by the brigands to look after their sheep. He locates and rescues Pastorella, and slays scores of brigands.

Canto XII

Calidore brings Pastorella to the Castle of Belgard, belonging to Sir Bellamoure who had been in love with Claribell, daughter of the Lord of Many Islands. Her father, disapproving of the match, had imprisoned her. But the lovers, by bribing the guards, had managed to have access to one another, and Claribell had borne Bellamoure a daughter. Her maid placed the child, who had a purple mole on her breast, in an open field, where it was found by a shepherd. After Claribell's parent died, the lovers were united and they lived happily. Pastorella stays at the castle, while Calidore continues his quest of the Blatant Beast.

One morning, Claribell's maid, attending Pastorella, helping to dress her, sees the mole she remembered on the abandoned child. She informs her mistress. Claribell, putting various pieces of information together, definitely identifies Pastorella as her long missing daughter!

Calidore finds the Blatant Beast despoiling a monastery, chasing the alarmed monks. Calidore has to fight him in the sacred Church itself. The beast shouts with a thousand tongues of various pitch - the sounds of dogs, cats, bears, tigers, humans, serpents-all full of slander for good and bad, high and low. Calidore works hard, lopping off some of the thousand heads, but for each one that falls, more grow. Finally, he muzzles the beast with tough iron links. He leads him captive through Faery Land, but eventually the animal breaks his iron bands, and is on the loose again when Canto XII ends.

THE FAERIE QUEENE

TEXTUAL ANALYSIS

THE MUTABILITY CANTOS

ANALYSIS

The Titaness, Mutability, perverts all that Nature had established first "in good estate." She breaks the laws of Nature, of Justice, of Policy. She is so bold as to demand that Cynthia, the moon-goddess, yield her throne to her, and, for a time, the light of the moon is dimmed. The lower world, deprived of light, appeals to Jove. Jove sends Mercury to order Mutability to cease molesting the moon, whereupon Mutability says she has no more regard for Jove's authority than she has for that of Cynthia. Jove summons a meeting of the gods to decide what course to follow with this presumptuous woman, "whether by open force or counsel wise." Mutability does not hesitate to walk boldly in at the council of the gods. As the granddaughter of Earth, the daughter of Chaos, this graceful and beautiful woman has an unquestionable ancestry. Jove, realizing that her ancestry presents strong claims, argues that the present race of gods holds heaven by sovereign might and the decree of eternal fate.

But Mutability appeals to the mother of gods and men, Nature herself. On Arlo's hill (Spenser's Irish home, about which he tells a mythological tale) the case is tried. "Ever young, yet full of age," "Dame" Nature hears the case. Mutability argues that even the earth, which seems unmoved and permanent, not a slave to mutability, yet changes in part–in her geographical features, in the very elements that compose her. She calls as witnesses the months themselves, the hours, even life and death. Who can deny that everything in the lower world is subject to Mutability? Pressing her case further, Mutability claims she can prove that the gods themselves are subject to change. She cites Cynthia, Mercury, Mars, even Jove himself. Nature's decision however, finds against Mutability's well argued case. Things, Nature says, are not changed from their first natures, though "by change their being do dilate" (spread out, grow). Things change superficially, but actually rule over the changes that they undergo.

In addition to the six completed books of *The Faerie Queene*, we have, in the words of the title used by Matthew Lownes in the 1609 Folio, "Two Cantos of Mutabilitie: Which, both for Forme and Matter, appear to be parcel of some following books of the Faerie Queene, Under the Legend of Constancie. Never before Imprinted." Where these cantos might have been designed to fit is a matter of dispute. Conceivably, they could have been written to fit into any suitable place in the following six books which were projected. Since their subject matter is so essentially philosophical (the relationship of "being" and "becoming"), underlying the other **themes** of *The Faerie Queene*, the cantos might even have been destined as a **climax** to the work. Conventionally, they are listed as Book VII, Cantos VI and VII.

THE SHEPHEARDE'S CALENDER

This follows the tradition of the pastoral as begun by Theocritus, Bion, and Virgil, and which was enormously popular in the Renaissance. In Theocritus the pastoral is still close to actual rural scenes and activities, but, in the course of its development it becomes highly conventionalized, and the rural framework is often a disguise for material containing social and political criticism. It is, of course, true that a poet can at any time return to something of the genuine simplicity of a Theocritus. Milton is aware of the two possibilities in the pastoral when, in the Lycidas, after a terrific outburst against corruption in the Anglican clergy, he invokes "the Sicilian muse" (Theocritus came from Sicily) to "return." A beautiful flower passage follows. On the other hand, in his attack on the clergy as bad pastors and "shepherds", Milton is fully in line with Renaissance tradition and with Spenser himself.

The pastoral of social criticism is written in a kind of code meant to be understood by "insiders." Direct criticism might invite prosecution or imprisonment if it were aimed at people in power. On the surface, the pastoral cannot be quoted as saying anything in "so many words." The real inner meaning of the pastoral of criticism is, therefore, always a matter of "digging." In Spenser's *Shephearde's Calender*, the "digging" is rendered particularly complex and difficult by the addition of a "gloss" (commentary) by "E. K." (identified as Edward Kirke). There is good reason to suspect that the gloss is meant to mislead as much as to clarify. If Paul McLane is right in arguing that the Rosalind of the pastoral is Queen Elizabeth, and that some rather forceful fire is turned on the proposed marriage of the Queen with the Duc d'Alencon, the necessity for this kind of gloss makes sense. This marriage, which at one moment seemed utterly certain, had been publicly opposed, and several people had been severely punished-one pamphleteer, John Stubbs, had had his right hand cut off!

E. K. classifies the "eclogues" (which are twelve in number, corresponding to the seasons of the year, starting with January) into plaintive (1, 6, 11, 12), moral (2, 5, 7, 9, 10), recreative (3, 4, 8). The "plaintive dialogues" contain "matter of love, or commendation of special personages." The "moral" dialogues are for the most part mixed with some satirical bitterness" (compare 7 and 9, dealing with dissolute shepherds and pastors, with Milton's Lycidas, and 10 dealing with "the contempt of poetry" with some of Milton's own remarks in his pastoral). E. K. does not bother to define what he means by the word "recreative." The March (3) Eclogue deals with a friend who has fallen in love; the April (4) Eclogue is a long lyrical piece in honor of Queen Elizabeth; the August (8) Eclogue is a traditional singing match between two shepherds. About the most significant characteristic these three eclogues have in common is the lack of personal involvement, and they may be "recreative" in the sense of "relaxing" rather than "moving" the reader.

Spenser's friends and patrons appear in the work. In the July (7) Eclogue, he praises Archbishop Grindal who advocated reforms within the framework of the Anglican church. In the November (11) Eclogue he calls Lobbin (the Earl of Leicester) "thou great shepherd." Roffyn (Bishop John Young) is portrayed as an ideal shepherd in the September (9) eclogue. Hobbinol, of course, in Spenser's lifelong confidant, Gabriel Harvey. Frequent references are made to Tityrus; when Tityrus is Roman, he is Virgil; when English, he is Chaucer.

In addition to expressing his political and religious alignments, Spenser makes bold experiments in language and versification in the *Calender*. He had been influenced by the "galaxy" of French poets (including Du Bellay, Ronsard, and others), the Pleiade, who were interested in extending and enlarging the French language so that it would be as fit a medium for creative expression as the classical languages, Greek and Latin. In his "Defence and Illustration of the French Language," Du Bellay advocates many of the practices that Spenser carries out. The language was not only to be enriched by borrowings from classical and foreign sources, but was to be revived by a judicious use of archaisms. This last feature of Spenser's style met with resistance, not only from Ben Jonson ("Spenser writ no language") but also from Sir Philip Sidney, a friend who singled out the *Calender* for praise. Sidney "dared not allow the same framing of his style in an old and rustic language." The playwright Thomas Nash, on the other hand, speaks of "the divine Master Spenser, the miracle of art, line for line for my life in the honor of England against Spain, France, Italy..."

THE COMPLAINTS CONTAINING SUNDRIE SMALL POEMS OF THE WORLD'S VANITIE (1591)

This volume (the poems are not "small" by modern standards of concentrated poetry) consists of the following: "The Ruines of Time"; "The Tears of the Muses"; "Virgil's Gnat" (a verse translation of the Culex); "Prosopopoia: Or Mother Hubberd's Tale"; "Ruines of Rome" (By Bellay); "Muiopotmos: Or The Fate of the Butterflie"; "Visions of the World's Vanitie"; "The Visions of Bellay"; "The Visions of Petrarch".

We shall briefly consider the poems in the order listed.

"The Ruines Of Time", dedicated to Lady Mary, Countess of Pembroke, sister of Sir Philip Sidney, is meant as a tribute to Sidney, who died in 1586. Among its **themes** is the power of time-a power to which empires and history must submit. Even Leicester could not escape:

He now is dead, and all his glorie gone, And all his greatnes vapoured to nought, That as a glasse upon the water shone...

Nor, of course, Sidney:

O noble spirite, live there ever blessed, The worlds late wonder, and the heavens new joy...

Spenser praises poetry which confers a kind of immortality:

And the immortal make, which els would die In foule forgetfulnesse, and nameless lie.

"The Teares of the Muses", dedicated to Lady Strange may have been written as early as 1580, though it was subsequently revised. Each of the Muses laments the state of English art and letters. It presents views analogous to those fashionable among the Pleiade. It repeats some of the ideas of the October Eclogue of the *Calender*; Spenser says that the poet is directly inspired by God, and thus the poet alone can confer immortality upon great men.

"Virgil's Gnat", "long since dedicated to the Earl of Leicester," is a paraphrase of the "pseudo-Virgilian" Culex. Both this and the "Muiopotmos" belong to a special kind of writing (derived from the Greek school of Alexandria) in which great weight and importance are attached to apparently trivial things. This work contains some autobiographical **allusions** believed to express Spenser's concern with Elizabeth's proposed d'Alencon marriage and its possible effect upon Spenser's patron, Leicester.

"Prosopopola: Or Mother Hubberd's Tale", dedicated to Lady Compton and Mountegle, like "Virgil's Gnat", belongs to an early period. It is a **satire** on court from 1577 to 1580, and follows medieval literary forms such as "the spectacle of fools," "the states (that is, social classes) of the world." It has a number of contemporary allusions. It touches upon Leicester's incurring the Queen's displeasure on learning from the French ambassador, Simier, of Leicester's secret marriage to the Countess of Essex, a woman thoroughly detested by the Queen, though she was her cousin. It expresses grave concern about the d' Alencon affair, and contains an attack upon Lord Burghley.

The "Ruines Of Rome" is a student translation of Du Bellay Antiquitez de Rome.

"Muiopotmos: Or The Fate of the Butterflie", dedicated to Lady Carey, is a fanciful and original work of the type of "Virgil's Gnat". Various effort have been made to interpret it as political allegory. in 1579 a feud broke out between Sir Philip Sidney, opposing French influence, and Lord Oxford, son-in-law of Burghley, who was supporting it. Clarion, the spider, would then be Burghley; Aragnoll, the butterfly, would be Sidney. This fanciful piece may deal with a later feud between Essex and Sir Walter Raleigh which led to the latter's departure for Ireland in 1589.

"Visions Of The World's Vanitie" consists of twelve **sonnets** in the Spenserian rhyming form (ababbcbccdcdee). The **theme** running through the collection is the power of the weak to injure the strong-for example, an ant upsetting an elephant by scurrying about in the beast's nostrils, or a worm destroying a giant cedar. These are exercises in the "emblem" literature of the period, and were often published with accompanying woodcuts.

"The Visions Of Bellay" And "The Visions Of Petrarch" are **sonnet** translations of Du Bellay's Songe and of Marot's own translation of Petrarch's sixth canzone. These are the earliest works, though they are printed last in the *Complaints* of 1591.

DAPHNAIDA, COLIN CLOUTS COME HOME AGAINE, AND ASTROPHEL

DAPHNAIDA

The "Daphnaida" (1591) is an **elegy** "upon the death of the noble and virtuous Douglas Howard, daughter and heir of Lord Howard, Viscount Byndon, and wife of Arthur Gorges, Esquire." Gorges was a sea captain and a kinsman of Sir Walter Raleigh. He served on Raleigh's expedition to the Azores in 1597. This **elegy**, dealing with Douglas, who was married at thirteen and who died at nineteen, is rather conventional and unimpassioned. Spenser to some extent imitates Chaucer's *Book of the Duchess*, but instead of Chaucer's octosyllabic couplets, this piece is composed in **rhyme** royal stanzas (ababcbc).

COLIN CLOUTS COME HOME AGAINE

Colin Clouts Come Home Againe (1595) narrates, in dialogue, Spenser's trip to England with Sir Walter Raleigh in 1589, and Spenser's subsequent impressions of the English court. It is in the tradition of the pastoral, but differs from *The Shephearde's Calender* in its clarity, its lack of recondite allusions. Several of the old figures appear again. Hobbinol (Gabriel Harvey) observes that the "woods and fields and floods revive" now that Spenser is back in England. Colin Clout (Spenser) describes how, when he was keeping his sheep "under the foot of Mole," he played his "pipes" (reeds), attracting the Shepherd of the Ocean (Sir Walter Raleigh). Cuddie (probably the poet Edward Dyer) asks what he sang about, and Spenser tells a mythological tale of his beloved Kilcolman countryside. Thestylis (our old friend, Lodowick Bryskett) congratulates him on the story, and asks about the "songs" of the other shepherd (Sir Walter Raleigh). Out of favor at court at the time, Sir Walter, in his songs, complains of "usage hard" by Cynthia, "the Ladie of the Sea" (Queen Elizabeth). The sea voyage back to England is described in heroic terms, the waves "rolling like mountains in wide wilderness." Spenser is delighted by his sight of England once again ("No nightly bodrags, nor no hue and cry"). They meet Elizabeth, whom Spenser deifies:

Her power, her mercy, and her wisedome, none Can deeme, but who the Godhead can define.

Through the offices of Sir Walter Raleigh, Elizabeth hears Spenser's verses. Spenser describes, with the names of shepherds, the men and women he admires. Thestylis wants to know why Colin, having enjoyed such happy experiences in London, would care to return to Ireland. Then follows some biting criticism of the court, to which reference is made in the first chapter of this book. Towards the end of the work, Colin speaks of Rosalind (here without doubt Queen Elizabeth), who is of "divine regard and heavenly hew" and who excels "all that ever eye did see."

ASTROPHEL

"Astrophel", dedicated to the Countess of Essex, who had been Sir Philip Sidney's widow, is a pastoral **elegy** upon the death of Sir Philip Sidney. It is the first of a collection of obituary poems, including two by Lodowick Bryskett, bound in the same volume with *Colin Clouts Come Home Againe*.

AMORETTI AND EPITHALAMION

The "Amoretti" form a sequence of eighty-eight sonnets. We are told how the poet tries to advance the cause of his love too quickly and is repulsed by the lady. A friend tells him he should be pushing on with *The Faerie Queene*, but love does not permit it. He writes the name of his love on the sands of the beach, but the ocean waves wipe it out. We are told that the suitor is a man of forty, wooing a woman superior to him in social rank. Slow to respond, the lady finally accepts him. Some critics regard the sequence as highly conventional and derivative. Others feel it has a convincing individuality. William Nelson in *The Poetry of Edmund Spenser* states: "To the casual modern reader, one Renaissance **sonnet** sequence seems muck like another. There is an inevitable sameness about these posies of love poems, inevitable because the long-established **convention** included not only a specific verse form but also a specified set of **themes** and subjects, like the pieces in chess, with which the sonneteer might play. The lover's unhappiness and unwavering devotion; the lady's heartlessness and beauty; the paradoxes of the inflamed lover and icy beloved, of painful joy and joyous pain; meditations on the moment of hope and the moment of despair; on time eyes, hair, jealousy, the perdurability of poetry-all these are to be found in the "Amoretti" as in other sonnet collections of the time." Professor Nelson is among those critics, however, who believe that Spenser transcended the mere **conventions** of the form.

A nearly unanimous acclaim greets the "Epithalamion" as one of the truly great poems of Renaissance literature. At times one may feel that Spenser, as a Renaissance humanist, tried to synthesize too many aspects of too many diverse traditions. In *The Faerie Queene* while one may see some of the cantos as works of genius, it is almost impossible not to regard others as the works of hard labor. But in the "Epithalamion", Spenser achieves the great union, the synthesis, which he has been aiming at in one way or another, with an exultant orchestration of great technical skill.

Spenser is dealing with a pivotal and unique experience of his own. The Muses have helped him to sing for others; now they must teach him to sing for himself. Like the great musician Orpheus, Spenser will sing for himself on the occasion of his marriage.

Hymen, the goddess of marriage, is awake on this beautiful morning, and everyone is dressed in his best. The girls are crowned with garlands. The Rosy morn has left Tithon's bed; the merry lark is greeting the morning sun; the three Graces are adorning the bride. Presently, she is ready to come forth on "the joyfulst day that ever sunne did see." Everyone is in a gay tumult, dancing, and singing the name of Hymen. In contrast to the excitement, the dignity of the bride is described; she has a religious seriousness; like St. Paul, she is engaged in the race toward the eternal truths:

Loe where she comes along with portly pace Lyke Phoebe from her chamber of the East, Arysing forth to run her mighty race, Clad all in white, that seems a virgin best.

Spenser is struck again by her physical beauty; did the merchant daughters ever see so fair a creature in their town before? Her spiritual beauty even exceeds her physical beauty. The poem moves with increasing impetuosity:

Open the temple gates unto my love, Open them wide that she may enter in, And all the postes adorne as doth behove, And all the pillours deck with girlands trim For to recyve this Saynt with honour dew, That commeth in to you.

The bride is brought home in victory; wine is to be poured out "without restraint or stay" - not by the cups, but "by the belly full."

At last the party is over. And a lyric dignity replaces the wild abandonment. "The bright evening star with golden crest" appears out of the East,

Fayre childe of beauty, glorious lampe of love...

Spenser thinks of the consummation of the marriage in terms of the Petrarchan oxymoron, "proud humility." He thinks of time and eternity, of the "high heavens, the temple of the gods," in which a thousand torches flame in the darkness of the night," and of a progeny that will merit "heavenly tabernacles." The movement of the poem has the ceremonial aspect of the masque, a form that Spenser loves and which is often reflected in *The Faerie Queene*, and this forms a successful tension with the underlying physical drive of the piece.

PROTHALAMION AND A VIEW OF THE PRESENT STATE OF IRELAND

PROTHALAMION

The "Prothalamion" (1596) is similar in structure to the "Epithalamion", using a key **refrain**, "Sweete Themmes, runne softly, till I end my song," which is similar to "The woods shall to me answer, and my echo ring." While it has a metrical excellence similar to that of Spenser's great poem, it lacks its passion of personal involvement. The two swans swimming softly down the Thames symbolize the double marriage of Lady Katherine Somerset, daughters of Edward Somerset, Earl of Worcester. It has a topographic review of some of the stately houses on the banks of the Thames, and mentions with touching pathos Leicester House.

A VIEW OF THE PRESENT OF IRELAND

A View Of The Present State Of Ireland (written between 1594 and 1597, but not published until 1633) is a prose dialogue between Eudoxus and Irenaeus (Spenser). Reference has already been made in the first chapter of this book to some of the thinking in this detailed report about Ireland. Spenser takes a rather narrow view of political contract. Once the leaders of a people have yielded their sovereignty to a view authority, the people cannot recover that sovereignty. And those who have rejected the laws imposed by the new authority cannot appeal to such laws. Such an attitude would, of course, leave the Irish with only one alternative, rebellion.

FOWRE HYMNES

Fowre Hymnes (1596), dedicated to Margaret, Countess of Cumberland, and to Mary, Countess of Warwick, wife of the brother of the Earl of Leicester, consist of two poems in honor of earthly love and beauty, and two in honor of heavenly love and beauty. The first two pieces are early work of Spenser's, and one of the ladies, probably the Countess of Warwick, who was something of a Puritan, had objected to their subject matter. Spenser is apparently making amends by his two new pieces dealing with "heavenly" love and beauty. These pieces reflect aspects of Plato's thinking, particularly in his Symposium, and the contributions of such Italian humanists as Marsilio Ficino, Giordano Bruno, Baldassare Castiglione, and Pico della Mirandola. The Hymns, while they may lack the conviction of Spenser's greatest poetry, are of particular interest to the historian of ideas. Spenser stresses the Platonic idea of love creating order out of chaos, imposing peace among warring elements, establishing a universal order. He follows the Greek "ladder of ascent" from the physical world to the transcendent world "essences," represented in turn by Cupid, Venus, Christ, God (the latter is aided by Sapience, or Wisdom, the "Queen of Heaven"). Spenser stops short of rejecting the physical world once "transcendent" perfection has been achieved; this is the point when man, in Greek thinking, ceases to have any dependence upon men. But Spenser was too attached to the tradition of chivalry and of personal human love to fully endorse the "other-worldliness" of the Platonic final destiny. He is the Platonist in making the soul alone essential, in making the body merely an instrument reflecting the soul:

For of the soule the bodie forme doth take: The soule is forme and doth the bodie make. (Hymne in Honour of Beautie, 132-3)

A beautiful body reflects a beautiful soul, though Spenser is wise enough to allow that accident may mar this equation. Heavenly Beauty is reflected in the world of the senses, but its essence is apart from them. The soul, when it comes to see heavenly beauty, is transported from the flesh, and here Spenser uses the key baroque word "ecstasy":

In which they sew such admirable things, As carries them into an extasy, And heare such heavenly notes, and carollings Of Gods high praise, that filles the brasen sky... (Hymne of Heavenly Beautie, 260.3)

CRITICAL COMMENTARY

THE CRITICS ON SPENSER

Spenserian criticism has, on the whole, followed a fairly consistent pattern over the years. At the time that Spenser wrote, criticism had not fully come into its own, either as an art or a science. Early references to Spenser are laudatory (William Webbe in A Discourse of English Poetry, 1586, Francis Meres in his Palladis Tamia, 1598), even when there are reservations about his use of language (Sir Philip Sidney, Ben Jonson). Through the seventeenth century Spenser's place in literature is assumed rather than discussed, though we have some admiring words from John Milton on Spenser as a moralist. The eighteenth century gives us important editions of the Spenser text (John Hughes in 1715, Thomas Warton's monumental work in 1754 and its subsequent edition in 1762). The nineteenth century is the age of capacious, if somewhat amateur, criticism such as that of William Hazlitt, and, nearer our own time, that of James Rusell Lowell and Edward Dowden. One of the main questions in this type of criticism is the importance that should be attached to the allegorical significance of *The Faerie Queene*. Hazlitt says that it can be conveniently disregarded. Lowell regards it as a set of beautiful pictures, only annoying when its morality becomes insistent. Dowden reaffirms the importance of Spenser's moral teaching as central to the work. The presentera, in which scientific and historical methods have been applied to literary research, has produced an enormous amount of critical literature on Spenser in the learned journals. More and more of his allegorical **allusions** have been pinned down, and the historical-philosophical background of his ideas has been explored. The study of comparative literature has defined nearly all Spenser's indebtedness of classical and continental sources. Most recently, the impact of the "new criticism," with its special emphasis on poetic **imagery** and symbolism, has led to a greatly revived interest in Spenser. Among important modern critics of Spenser are the following (some of their works are included in the attached bibliography): Leicester Bradner, B. E. C. Davis, Edwin Greenlaw, A. C. Hamilton, A. C. Judson, E. Legouis, Paul E. McLane, William Nelson, M. Pauline Parker, Isabel E. Rathbone, W. L. Renwick, E. de Selincourt, Virgil K. Whitaker. A standard variorum edition of Spenser's works has been brought out by the John Hopkins University Press, 10 vols. in 11, 1932-57.

To mark a certain historical progression in Spenser criticism, as well as to offer some provocative statements, especially in regard to *The Faerie Queene*, a number of quotations are attached below in chronological order.

William Webbe (1586): "Sorry I am that I cannot find none other with whom I might couple him (Spenser) in this catalogue..."

John Milton, "Areopagitica", 1644: "That virtue therefore which is but a youngling in the contemplation of evil, and knows not the utmost that vice promises to her followers, and rejects it, is but a blank virtue, not a pure; her whiteness is but an excremental whiteness; which was the reason why our sage and serious poet Spenser, whom I dare be known to think a better teacher than Scotus or Aquinas, describing true temperance under the person of Guyon, brings him in with his palmer through the cave of Mammon and the bower of earthly bliss, that he might see and know, and yet abstain."

John Dryden, *Essay On **Satire***, 1692: There is no uniformity in the design of Spenser; he aims at the accomplishment of no one action; he raises up a hero for every one of his adventures; and endows each of them with some particular moral virtue, which renders them all equal, without subordination or preference."

Thomas Rymer, *A Short View Of The Tragedy Of The Last Age*, 1663: "Spenser may be reckoned the first of our heroic poets. He had a large spirit, a sharp perhaps above poetry, perhaps above any that ever wrote since Virgil, but our misfortune is, he wanted a true idea, and lost himself by following an unfaithful guide. Though, besides Homer and Virgil, he had read Tasso, yet he rather allowed himself to be misled by Ariosto, with whom, blindly rambling on marvels and adventures, he makes no conscience of probability; all is fanciful and chimerical, without any uniformity, or without any foundation in truth; in a word his poem is perfect Fairy-Land."

Joseph Addison, *Spectator*, No. 419, 1712: "There is another sort of imaginary beings, that we sometimes meet with among poets, when the author represents any passion, appetite, virtue, or vice, under a visible shape, and makes it a person or actor in his poem. Of this nature are the descriptions of Hunger and Envy in Ovid, of Fame in Virgil, and of Sin and Death in Milton. We find a whole creation of the like shadowy persons in Spenser, who had an admirable talent in representations of this kind."

Dr. Samuel Johnson, *The Rambler*, No. 121, 1752: "His (Spenser's) style was in his own time allowed to be vicious, so darkened with old words and peculiarities of phrase, and so remote from common use, that Jonson bodly pronounces him to have written no language. His **stanza** is at once difficult and unpleasing; tiresome to the ear by its uniformity, and to the attention by its length. It was at first formed in imitation of the Italian poets, without due regard to the genius of our language."

Thomas Warton, *Observations On The Fairy Queen Of Spenser*, 1754: "His poetry is the careless exuberance of a warm imagination and a strong sensibility. It was his business to engage the fancy, and to interest the attention by bold and striking images, in the formation and the disposition of which, little labor or art was applied. The various and the marvelous were the chief sources of delight."

Oliver Goldsmith, 1759: "With all his faults, no poet enlarges the imagination more than Spenser."

William Wordsworth, *The Prelude*, Book III, 1795-1805:

Sweet Spenser, moving through his clouded heaven, With the moon's beauty, and the moon's soft pace, I call him Brother, Englishman, and Friend!

William Hazlitt, *Lectures On The English Poets*, 1818: [Spenser's verse] "is the perfection of melting harmony, dissolving the soul in pleasure, or holding it captive in the chains of suspense. Spenser was the poet of our waking dreams; and he has invented not only a language, but a music of his own for them. The undulations are infinite, like those of the waves of the sea; but the effect is still the same, lulling the senses into a deep oblivion of the jarring noises of the world, from which we have no wish to be ever recalled."

Percy Bysshe Shelley, *A Defence Of Poetry*, 1821: "Those in whom the poetical faculty, though great, is less intense, as Euripedes, Lucan, Tasso, Spenser, have frequently affected a moral aim, and the effect of their poetry is diminished in exact proportion to the degree in which they compel us to advert to this purpose."

Thomas Babington Macaulay, 1830: "Nay, even Spenser himself, though assuredly one of the greatest poets who ever lived, could not succeed in the attempt to make allegory interesting. . . .One unpardonable fault, the fault of tediousness, pervades the whole of The Fairy Queen."

Leigh Hunt, *Imagination And Fancy*, 1844: "Take him in short for what he is, whether great or less than his fellows, the poetical faculty is so abundantly and beautifully predominant in him above every other, though he had passion, and thought, and plenty of ethics, and was as learned a man as Ben Jonson, perhaps as Milton himself, that he has always been felt by his countrymen to be what Charles Lamb called him, the 'poet's poet.' "

James Russell Lowell, in an article in the *North American Review*, April, 1875: "In the world into which Spenser carries us there is neither Time nor Space, or rather it is outside and independent of both, and so is purely ideal, or, more truly imaginary; yet it is full of form, color, and all earthly luxury, and so far, if not real, yet apprehensible by the senses. There are no men and women in it, yet it throngs with airy and immortal shapes that have the likeness of men and women, and hint at some kind of foregone reality." "The true use of Spenser is as a gallery of pictures which we visit as the mood takes us, and where we spend an hour or two at a time, long enough to sweeten our perceptions, not so long as to cloy them." "Whenever in The

Fairy Queen you come suddenly on the moral, it gives you a shock of unpleasant surprise, a kind of grit, as when one's teeth close on a bit of gravel in a dish of strawberries and cream" (compare Shelley's view above).

Edward Dowden, Spenser, *The Poet And Teacher*, 1875, asks regarding Lowell's remarks above, whether "we shall accept this view, or that of a Milton - 'a better teacher than Scotus or Aquinas'?" "How, then, should we read The Fairy Queen? Is it poetry? Or is it philosophy?. . . .Are we merely to gaze on with wide-eyed expectancy as at a marvelous pageant or procession, in which knights and ladies, Saracers and wizards, antiks and wild men pass before our eyes?. . . .The special virtue of The Fairy Queen will be found only by one who receives it neither as pageantry nor as philosophy, but in the way in which Spenser meant that it should be received - as a living creature of the imagination, a spirit incarnate, 'one altogether,' of a reasonable soul and human flesh subsisting."

E. Legouis, *Edmund Spenser*, 1923: "His Fairy Queen might be described as a poetic rendering of the masques of his time, which made that short-lived enchantment immortal by transcribing it into verse. It was to keep the masque's gorgeous scenery, the scenic movement and changes, the actors' gestures and mimicry. He was, moreover, to reproduce the alternatives of masque and antimasque, that is, of the beautiful and grotesque. Lastly, he gives an equivalent for the stage music in his harmonious stanza."

M. Pauline Parker, *The Allegory Of The Faerie Queene*, 1960: "It is not surprising that Spenser should have conceived his greatest work as a 'continued allegory or dark conceit.' That was the traditional and well-approved way of expounding moral truth. But also *The Faerie Queene* had to be an allegory. There is no other way of making a story about immaterial things."

William Nelson, *The Poetry Of Edmund Spenser,* 1963: "For none of the books of *The Faerie Queene*, therefore, is a true conclusion possible. The powers of darkness may for a time be held prisoner, seen in their true horror and rendered impotent, but since they are of earth's essence they will again break free and threaten destruction, night, and chaos. Despite the ever-present threat, indeed because of it, the created world remains beautiful, various, and fecund, and man may hope that when his own strength cannot avail to keep it so, the grace of God will come to his aid. So much of victory is all that can be expected as long as the Red Cross Knight serves Gloriana and Mutabilitie fulfills her natural function. Beyond, and really beyond the bounds of *The Faerie Queene*, St. George unites forever with Una in the final Sabbath when all things rest upon the pillars of Eternity."

ESSAY QUESTIONS AND ANSWERS

....

The answers to the following review and discussion questions are contained, generally speaking, in the chapters or cantos referred to, except where the reader is directed to such common reference works as the *Encyclopedia Britannica*, the *Dictionary of National Biography*, or histories of literature, for further material.

The second part consist of key essay discussion questions and detailed answers.

LIFE AND ENVIRONMENT

1. By reference to the *Dictionary of National Biography*, identify the following, mentioning their characteristic activities and achievements: Richard Mulcaster, Archbishop Edmund Grindall, Gabriel Harvey, Lord Grey of Wilton, Sir Francis Walsingham, William Cecil (Lord Burghley).

2. What was the function of the "undertakers" in Ireland?

3. What autobiographical references to Spenser's life are contained in *Colin Clouts Come Home Againe?*

4. What attitude towards the Irish does Spenser take in *A View of The Present State of Ireland?*

5. With what noble house was Spenser associated by family ties? Who were the three influential ladies connected with it?

6. Read the article on Sir Philip Sidney in the *Dictionary of National Biography?* Why was he considered the "first gentleman of his time".

7. By consulting a history of English Literature (e.g. the Cambridge History), explain the importance of Sir Philip Sidney's *Defence of Poetry.*

8. Explain the relationship of Spenser to Sir Walter Raleigh.

9. By consulting the *Encyclopedia Britannica* or the *Dictionary of Biography*, explain the importance of Sir Walter Raleigh in Elizabethan history.

THE FAERIE QUEENE: INTRODUCTION

1. What part does Lodowick Bryskett play in Spenser's life and affairs?

2. What was the over-all purpose of *The Faerie Queene*?

3. What is meant by the humanist ideal of the complete man?

4. What is the difference between ethical and political virtues?

5. What was the Aristotelian idea of virtue?

6. How extensive was Spenser's entire project for *The Faerie Queene?*

7. How much of the project was actually accomplished?

8. What was the Renaissance meaning of glory?

9. What was meant by the virtues of Magnificence?

10. How would you distinguish "Glory" from "Magnificence"?

11. Why could not Spenser simply repeat the Aristotelian classification of the virtues?

12. What books in *The Faerie Queene* correspond fairly closely to Aristotle's classification of the virtues? Which do not?

13. What advantage does Spenser find in presenting moral teaching in the form of poetry?

14. On what levels does Spenser's allegory operate?

15. What are some of the characteristics of the "atmosphere" of *The Faerie Queene?*

16. Why may the words "masque" and "tableau" be applied to *The Faerie Queene?*

17. What is meant by a "night errant"?

18. What were the ideals of medieval Knighthood?

19. In what way is Spenser sometimes pessimistic?

20. In what way does Spenser present an "ideal" world in *The Faerie Queene?*

21. What was the function of the poet according to Spenser?

22. Locate a half-dozen Homeric **similes** in Spenser.

23. What is the artistic effect of th Spenserian **stanza** in *The Faerie Queene?*

24. name a principal reason for some of the odd characteristics of Spenser's language.

THE FAERIE QUEENE: BOOK I

1. What is meant by the word "legend" attached to the titles of the various books?

2. What kind of truth is symbolized by Una?

3. Why does the Red Cross Knight signify "the Church Militant"?

4. What is symbolized by the dwarf?

5. How does Spenser describe Error?

6. Why should the Red Cross Knight have to defeat nights with the names Sansfoy, Sansloy, Sansjoy?

7. Can you think of an explanation of why Lucifera's palace is built on sand (Canto IV)? See Luke 6:48-49.

8. Why would you meet a Sansjoy ("without joy") in Lucifera's palace? Does Spenser mean that joy must be related to faith and law?

9. Explain how Prince Arthur (Canto VII) is of decisive aid at a critical point in the affairs of the Red Cross Knight.

10. How does Spenser present Despair (Canto IX)? In what ways might you consider the allegory effective.

11. Describe the training of the Red Cross Knight at the House of Holiness.

12. What sources of interest does Spenser create in describing the fight between the Red Cross Knight and the dragon?

THE FAERIE QUEENE: BOOK II

1. What is meant by Temperance?

2. What is the function of the Palmer in Book II?

3. Show how Medina (Canto II) presents "the golden mean."

4. Show how Spenser exhibits a sense of humor and of comedy in in his portrayal of Braggadocchio (Canto III).

5. Trace the consequences of Sir Guyon sparing the life of Pyrochles in Canto V.

6. What approach to life is represented by Phaedria (Canto VI)?

7. Are there any reasons to consider the allegory of the Cave of Mammon particularly effective (Canto VII)?

8. What are Sir Guyon's reactions to Mammon's vision of wealth?

9. What are the magic properties of Arthur's sword (Canto VIII)?

10. How does Arthur intervene at a critical point in Guyon's affairs in Canto VIII (compare also Book I, Canto VII, where Arthur aids the Red Cross Knight)?

11. What forces are symbolized in the conflict between Maleger and Alma (Canto XI)?

12. Why does Spenser stress "the artificial" in the Bower of Bliss?

13. Distinguish between the true Genius (Book III, vi) and the false Genius here in Canto XII.

14. What principal **themes** are presented in the Bower of Bliss?

THE FAERIE QUEENE: BOOK III

1. What conditions did Malecasta impose as her "custom" of the castle?

2. How did Britomart come to fall in love with Artegall (Canto II)? Britomart and Artegall (Canto III)?

3. What befalls Marinell after he has been seriously wounded by Britomart (Canto IV)?

4. Describe the relationship of Belphoebe and Timias (Canto V).

5. Show how Spenser in the Garden of Adonis (Canto VI) constructs an allegory emphasizing married as well as virginal chastity.

6. Explain the situation leading to the creation of the False Florimell (Canto VIII).

7. What are the "perils" of the True Florimell (Canto VIII)? What do you think they illustrate?

8. What are the comic elements of the Malbecco-Hellenore story (Canto IX and X)?

9. In what ways is the Malbecco story "tragic"?

10. What forces are present in the "Masque of Cupid" that should be absent in a chaste love?

11. Contrast the presentation of Cupid as an evil force here (Canto XIII) with Cupid as a good force in Canto VI, and in Book IV, x.

THE FAERIE QUEENE: BOOK IV

1. How does Spenser illustrate unstable and unproductive "friendships" in Canto I?

2. What events led Triamond to marry Canacee (Canto III)?

3. Under what circumstances does Britomart actually recognize Arthur for the first time (Canto VI)?

4. How are Belphoebe and Timias brought together after a long separation (Canto VIII)?

5. How does Slander extend hospitality to Arthur, Amoret, Aemylia (Canto VIII)?

6. What kinds of distortions of love are symbolized in Druon, Claribell, Blandamour, Paridell, the False Florimell (Canto IX)?

7. Why did Scudamour succeed in passing successfully through all the hazards in the Temple of Venus?

8. What event led to Marinell's change of heart about Florimell?

THE FAERIE QUEENE: BOOK V

1. Analyze Spenser's presentation of the "giant of Communism" (Canto II).

2. Show how "false pity" betrayed Sir Artegall in his conflict with the giantess Radigund (Canto V).

3. Explain the meaning of the Allegory in the Temple of Isis (Canto VII).

4. How do Prince Arthur and Sir Artegall meet (Canto VIII)? Does Arthur have to render aid as in previous cases of first meeting with principal knights?

5. Consult the Encyclopedia Britannica to determine the events that led to the execution of Mary Queen of Scots (also Duessa).

6. By consulting available reference books see what significant facts you can discover about Henry IV of Navarre (1589-1610), and about any Spanish landings in Ireland during Spenser's lifetime.

THE FAERIE QUEENE: BOOK VI

1. What outstanding examples of courtesy, and of its gross violations, can be found in the first three cantos?

2. What do you think Spenser intended by his portrayal of the "salvage man" (Canto IV)?

3. Can Arthur's sparing of Sir Turpine (Canto VI) be classified as "false pity? Is Spenser pointing out a similar danger here as in Sir Guyon's sparing the life of Pyrochles (II, v), and in Sir Artegall's leniency in regard to Radigund (IV, v)?

4. What lesson in regard to Courtesy is Spenser driving home in the allegory of Mirabella (Canto VI and VII)?

5. What contrast is presented between the "salvage man" and the salvage nation of Canto VIII?

6. Can you point out the difference between a pastoral eclogue and a pastoral romance? One important difference is that the romance has a definite story line, and its meaning is not disguised. What do you think "pastorals" have in common?

7. In what significance can be attached to the fact that Calidore could not actually kill the Blatant Beast?

OTHER WORKS OF SPENSER

1. What are the characteristics of the Spenserian eclogue?

2. What were some of the objectives of the Pleiade?

3. In what way were some of the principles of the Pleiade echoed in the October Eclogue and in "The Tears of the Muses"?

4. What reasons might be given for acclaiming the "Epithalamion" as one of the great poems of the Renaissance?

5. What ideas derived from Plato are to be found in the *Fowre Hymnes?*

6. Using the section, "The Critics on Spenser," show how critics have differed on the value of the moral element in *The Faerie Queene.*

ESSAY DISCUSSION QUESTIONS AND ANSWERS

Question: How Effective Is Spenser's Allegorical Method?

Answer: In answering this question, we have first to recognize two things. One is the fact that the allegorical method is generally unfamiliar to the modern reader, and he may mistake his initial difficulties with allegory as some sort of artistic clumsiness on the part of the poet. Secondly, we have to allow for the fact that the total projected work of Spenser would have run to twenty-four books, of which only six were completed. We can only infer what total orchestration Spenser might have created from his immense design.

Quotations from Spenser critics included in this book indicate a traditional division of point of view on this subject. A Milton, an Edward Dowden, a Pauline Parker, a William Nelson accept the moral allegory as containing the essence of the work. A Thomas Rymer, a Shelley, a Macaulay, a James Russell Lowell cannot take the central allegory very seriously. They may be prepared to accept a "faerie" world of rich poetry, but cannot respond to the moral earnestness of the work. The tendency of present day Spenser scholarship is to give increased attention to the inner meanings of Spenser's moral philosophy. There are two reasons for this. One results from the contemporary interest in "levels of meaning." Certain modern writers who have generated great interest (a James Joyce, a Kafka) are themselves allegorists, and Spenser has benefited from the desire to explore "multiple meaning." The other reason has been the increasing study of the History of Ideas and of Comparative Literature. The background of Spenser's philosophy in medieval tradition, as modified by Protestant and Humanist thought, particularly by Neoplatonism, has been the subject of repeated sensitive analysis.

As we have noted in the Introduction, Spenser does not closely adhere to Aristotle's classification of the virtues. The virtues listed by Aristotle are Courage, Temperance, Liberality, Magnificence, Magnanimity, Love of Honor, Gentleness, Truthfulness, Urbanity, Friendliness, Modesty, Righteous Indignation. In the Republic, Plato lists four "Cardinal" Virtues (cardinal is derived from a Latin word meaning a door-hinge - the cardinal virtues are those on which all the other virtues "hang" or depend): Courage, Temperance, Wisdom, Justice. It is obviously easier to make clear cut distinctions between the virtues in a prose philosophical treatise than in a long imagistic poem, even when the latter's humanistic objective is "to teach" as well as "to delight." In addition, Spenser has complicated the Aristotelian picture by certain complex Christian theological ideas.

Spenser's allegory cannot be considered effective if it were to be narrowly judged as a kind of illustrated textbook of Aristotle Aristotle's "speaking picture." But this is no way to judge the work. Though a close examination will show some real inconsistencies and loose ends in *The Faerie Queene.* they are like those in Shakespeare's plays, of a minor sort that really have to be dug out to be observed. What may appear to be inconsistencies often have a very convincing allegorical explanation. Thus "natural reason" is a dwarf in Book I where reason is related to Holiness (the Red Cross Knight, but in book II reason is presented by the Palmer who is at least on an equal footing with the virtue of Temperance (Sir Guyon). Some of the "ambiguities" of the allegory are also easily understandable in Spencer's insistent contrast between the true and the counterfeit, and in his constant stress upon weakness even in the good and strong, sometimes even betrayed by false pity, as in the case of Sir Guyon and of Sir Artegall

Question: What Is Meant By Neoplatonism In Spenser?

Answer: Neoplatonism, originally associated with the third century philosopher, Plotinus, widely influenced Italian humanists of the Renaissance, particularly Marsilio Ficino and the Florentine Academy. Neoplatonism lent itself to various mythological developments, but its essential characteristics are fairly easy to describe. It is concerned with the relationship of multiplicity to unity, and with the idea of love as the motivating power in the universe. All emanates from the One. The unitary intellect of the One ("Nous" - Greek for "mind") radiates the "seminal reasons" (cf. Shakespeare's "nature's germens") upon "soul." Anima Mundi ("the soul of the world") is thought to possess the forming ideas which give identity to matter (cf. Shakespeare's "the soul of the wide world dreaming on things to come"). The seminal reasons stand between the One and the Many. The many constitute the world of corporeality. These seminal reasons, these forming principles, enter the material world through a meeting of their own impulses with the right external circumstances (this is described in Spenser's Garden of Adonis, Book III, vi). The corporeal world is a reflection of the spiritual world of the One. The whole process of emanation is one of Divine necessity, rather than of choice. Through "love" everything has an impulse to go in a certain direction, and all things are in a sense united by an overriding purpose or "order." The "One" is identified with the essence of heavenly beauty, reflected in the reality of an earthly beauty discernible by the senses, though not comparable to the heavenly beauty. Truth is an aspect of this heavenly beauty known only to the soul; holiness is a condition of the soul by which the beauty of truth can be known and loved.

Neoplatonism retains the basic idea (found in Plato) of a ladder of ascent, of perfection. Undoubtedly, this concept of continuing aspiration through love was one of psychological attractions of Neoplatonism for Renaissance thinkers. It is the carefully worked out scheme of Spencer's *Fowre Hymnes.* The Neoplatonic ladder had five stages of aspiration. First, the lover awakens his senses to bodily beauty. Secondly, the realization is developed that beauty of the mind is greater than that of the body. Thirdly, an awareness is born that the beauty of the beloved is a memory of a previous heavenly existence. Fourthly, a universal concept of womanly beauty is attained. Lastly, a perception of heavenly beauty itself is formed, an approach to the Divine essence. Love ends in Nous, the possession of the one.

Neoplatonism affects Spenser, Shakespeare, Milton in different ways and with different modifications. Obviously, while some aspects of Neoplatonism might be harmonious with Christian doctrine, other aspects were hard to reconcile. In Spenser, the most complete adaptation of Neoplatonism, outside the *Fowre Hymnes*, is to be found in the Garden of Adonis, Canto VI of Book III of *The Faerie Queene* (for a detailed analysis see William Nelson, *The Poetry of Edmund Spenser*, pp. 206-23). Spenser is careful to restrict the idea of reincarnation (present in many interpretations of Neoplatonism) in the Garden of Adonis to "form" but not to "soul," though elsewhere he equates the two. He thus avoids an overt contradiction of Christianity. Shakespeare, in his sonnets, adopts the Neoplatonic idea of beauty, but insists on the value of the material world by arguing that it is the duty of a beautiful woman to have offspring, that thereby beauty's rose will never die. If Dennis Saurat is correct in *Milton: Man and Thinker*, Milton's picture of Christ in *Paradise Lost* is deeply affected by Neoplatonism. Christ is there portrayed as the creator of the world and of the angels (without scriptural support), the victor over Satan's army - the active principle emanating from the "One," God the Father. The Son is an "emanation" of the Father rather than being one with Him as in the traditional doctrine of the Trinity.

Question: What Are Spenser's Religious Views?

Answer: A consensus among the critics hold that Spenser's religious views were those of a "conservative" Protestant. The medieval atmosphere of *The Faerie Queene* is presented with a nostalgic sympathy, though he presents Corceca (*The Faerie Queene*, I iii) and Archimago is using Catholic devotions in a superstitious or hypocritical way. Like Milton, he takes Roman Catholic "wickedness" for granted. But his opposition to Catholicism as well as to abuses in the Church of England (*The Shephearde's Calender*) reveals rather the ethical zeal of the reformer than a strong rejection of Catholic tradition. It must be remembered that the Church of England in Spenser's time retained a great portion of the body of Catholic doctrine, a fact that was to lead to powerful attacks upon it by more "radical" Protestants, the Calvinists, and, eventually, in the seventeenth century, to civil war. Insofar as *The Faerie Queene* has a Protestant doctrinal cast, it lies in the assumption of "election" ("predestination") by the principal characters. The Red Cross Knight, Sir Artegall are "chosen" for salvation. In contrast to Catholic tradition, where the freedom of the "natural" man to choose (to cooperate with Grace or not) has an important place, Spenser stresses Grace alone. Stress is placed, in the words of William Nelson, "upon human folly and weakness and divine omniscience and omnipotence." With the possible exception of Poeana (*The Faerie Queene*, IV, ix) and of the Sir Enias who had been misled by Sir Turpine (VI, vii), Spenser does not portray acts of contrition and of remorse as, for example, a Shakespeare does. People remain what they are. Of course, some allowance has to be made for the fact that they are also allegorical figures. The virtues have to remain constant, and so do their allegorical alternatives. Spenser softens the assurance of the elect by showing that they have to go through a process of education and development (the Red Cross Knight in the House of Holiness, Sir Guyon in the House of Temperance, Serena and Timias under the guidance of the hermit).

Question: What Characterizes Spenser As A Narrative Artist?

Answer: Spenser draws on a vast variety of sources for his material. Undoubtedly this use of sources was a source of pleasure for the Elizabethan readers. They enjoyed in English adaptation of material they had recognized in other languages, and speculated about Spenser's deliberate changes and re-arrangements in such material. As one critic observes, "the Legend of Holiness is the life of a saint, and imitatio Christi; the Legend of Chastity is notably in Ariosto's manner; the Legend of Courtesy has the character of a pastoral romance." Just as there is a variety of verse experimentation in *The Shephearde's Calender*, so there is a variety of narrative technique in *The Faerie Queene*. We can have a completely told short story, carefully worked out from the statement of conflict to the final **climax** as in the Malbecco - Hellenore-Paridell triangle (Book III, ix & x); we can have a romantic allegory, an "inset" completed in one Canto as in Scudamour's description of the winning of Amoret (Book IV, x). In his longer narrative sequences Spencer deliberately interrupts a story when it comes to a point of high tension, by crossing it with another sequence that had, in its turn, been also interrupted. This is a device to maintain suspense, though it may also have an irritating effect on some readers who want to see one thing through at a time, especially, if the two or more sequences are not tightly knit to one another. When a reader has become more accustomed to the multiplicity of Spenser's figures, this technique of interrupted narrative is much easier to accept. Spenser's stories run much more effectively on a repeated reading. Spenser relieves the intensity of the allegory by humor and comic incident, as we indicate below.

Question: Does Spenser Have A Sense Of Humor?

Answer: Even in Shakespeare there is no guarantee that what the dramatist thought was funny would appear funny to everyone today. But the sometimes repeated allegation that Spenser, like John Milton, has no sense of humor arises more from a prejudice against an overt moralist than from an actual reading of the text. His humor is frequently "sardonic" ("bitterly ironic") as in his portrayal of Braggadocchio and Trompart; these clowns are funny, but we are meant to despise them. Spenser's humor does not have the lightness of touch coming from good will toward its subject (as in Shakespeare's portrayal of Falstaff); it has a constantly satiric bite. A good example is that of Gryll, at the end of Book II of *The Faerie Queene*, the man who resents his rescue by Sir Guyon from the Bower of Bliss, for he prefers being a pig to being a man. Spenser occasionally uses a humorous anecdotal story as an "inset" to his main narrative. Such is the cynical story told by the Squire of Dames (Book III, vii) about the chastity of women. Spenser's humor is mordant, in one key, that of a satirist (this is true of all his works), but it is dominant enough to be an essential part of his artistic method.

BIBLIOGRAPHY AND GUIDE TO FURTHER RESEARCH

LIFE

Judson, A. C., *The Life of Edmund Spenser* (Baltimore, 1945). Considered a definitive life of Spenser; meant to be supplementary and complementary to the Variorum Edition.

GENERAL

Bradner, Leicester, *Edmund Spenser and The Faerie Queene* (Chicago, 1948). A successful effort to bring *The Faerie Queene* to the educated general reader; very useful for students.

Cory, Robert Ellsworth, *Edmund Spenser: A Critical Study* (Berkeley, 1917). A fairly complete treatment of the whole of Spenser, a little old-fashioned in content and style.

Davis, B. E. C., *Edmund Spenser: A Critical Study* (New York, 1962). A general critical work, emphasizing poetic style and intellectual ideas.

Nelson, William, *The Poetry of Edmund Spenser* (Columbia, 1963). A penetrating book of general criticism, frequently eloquent.

BACKGROUND OF IDEAS

Bhattacherje. M., *Platonic Ideas in Spenser*, foreword by E. Legouis (New York, 1935). Emphasizes Italian applications of Plato, as in Giordano Bruno, Pico della Mirandola.

Ellrodt, Robert, *Neoplatonism in the Poetry of Spenser* (Geneva, 1962). A quite readable doctoral thesis; an exhaustive treatment of the subject.

Legouis, E., *Edmund Spenser* (Paris, 1923). Six readable lectures, stressing ideas and values, given at John Hopkins University, 1922.

Rathbone, Isabel E., *The Meaning of Spenser's Fairyland* (Columbia, 1937). Traces the literary and historical background of gods and heroes in Spenser's fairyland.

Whitaker, Virgil K., *The Religious Basis of Spenser's Poetry* (Stamford, 1950). A short book (about 70 pages) arguing that Spenser's religious outlook is that of a conservative Anglican.

SOURCES AND STYLE

Arthos, John, *On the Poetry of Spenser and the Form of the Romances* (London, 1956). A deftly written account of Spenser's relationship to his Italian sources.

Hughes, Merritt Y., *Virgil and Spenser* (Berkeley, 1929). Treats the influence of Virgil on Spenser; also some consideration of Du Bellay and Ronsard.

Renwick, W. L., *Edmund Spenser: An Essay in Renaissance Poetry* (London, 1925). Particularly emphasizes style, meter, structure in Spenser's works, with special reference to the new poetry of the sixteenth century.

Satterthwaite, Alfred W., *Spenser, Ronsard and Du Bellay: A Renaissance Comparison* (Princeton, 1960). A study in comparative literature with particular emphasis on Platonism in Spenser, Du Bellay, Ronsard.

HISTORY

Greenlaw, Edwin, *Studies in Spenser's Historical Allegory* (Baltimore, 1932). This is a John Hopkins monograph in literary history. It includes four papers, containing "Spenser and the Earl of Leicester."

Henley, P., *Spenser in Ireland* (Cork, 1938). Contains interesting historical data.

ALLEGORICAL INTERPRETATION

Hamilton, A. C., *The Structure of the Allegory in The Faerie Queene* (Oxford, 1961). A very complete treatment of the moral aspects of the allegory.

Parker, M. Pauline, *The Allegory of The Faerie Queene* (Oxford, 1960). A penetration in depth of the meaning of *The Faerie Queene* by a sensitive Spenser enthusiast.

Smith, Charles G., *Spenser's Theory of Friendship* (Baltimore, 1935). A short essay helpful in interpreting Book IV of *The Faerie Queene*.

Spens, Janet, *Spenser's Fairy Queen: An Interpretation* (London, 1934). A short, highly personal interpretation, with a special theory about the seven deadly sins as the basis of the allegory.

ABOUT SPECIAL POEMS

McLane, Paul E., *Spenser's Shephearde's Calender* (Notre Dame, 1961). The most comprehensive account of the possible concealed historical meanings in the work.

Hieatt, A. K., *Short Times Endless Monument: The Symbolism of the Numbers in Edmund Spenser's Epithalamion* (Columbia, 1960). A new and interesting theory in a Columbia doctoral dissertation.

ON SPENSER LITERARY CRITICISM

1. Mueller, William R., *Spenser's Critics: Changing Currents in Literary Taste* (Syracuse, 1959). A highly readable set of extracts showing trends in Spenser criticism.

2. Wurtzbaugh, Jewel, *Two Centuries of Spenserian Scholarship* (1609-1805), Baltimore, 1936. Discusses editions and critical "climates."

REFERENCE WORKS

Atkinson, D. F., *Edmund Spenser: A Bibliographical Supplement* (Baltimore, 1937). An annotated bibliography of books and articles then in existence (1937) dealing with Edmund Spenser.

Carpenter, F. I., *A Reference Guide to Edmund Spenser* (Chicago, 1925). For names, allegorical meanings, cross-references.

Greenlaw et al, *Variorum Edition of Edmund Spenser*, 10 v. in 11, (Baltimore, 1932-57). The definitive edition of Spenser.

Jones, H. S. V., *A Spenser Handbook* (New York, 1930). This has had several subsequent printings. Useful for bibliographies, particularly to articles, at the end of chapters.

Lotspeich, H.G., *Classical Mythology in the Poetry of Edmund Spenser* (Princeton, 1932). Contains an alphabetical listing of classical allusions and sources.

McNeir, Waldo F. & Foster Provost, *Annotated Bibliography of Edmund Spenser*, 1937-1960, Duquesne Philological Series 3 (Pittsburg, 1962). Brings the Spenser bibliography up to 1960 from 1937 where Atkinson left off.

Osgood, C.G., *A Concordance to the Poems of Edmund Spenser* (Washington, 1915). Indispensable for advanced study of Spenser, compiled by one of the Variorum editors.

www.ingramcontent.com/pod-product-compliance
Lightning Source LLC
LaVergne TN
LVHW021713060526
838200LV00050B/2649